St. Leonard of Port Maurice

The Hidden Treasure

Or the Immense Excellence of the Holy Sacrifice of the Mass ...

St. Leonard of Port Maurice

The Hidden Treasure
Or the Immense Excellence of the Holy Sacrifice of the Mass ...

ISBN/EAN: 9783743484047

Manufactured in Europe, USA, Canada, Australia, Japa

Cover: Foto ©Lupo / pixelio.de

Manufactured and distributed by brebook publishing software (www.brebook.com)

St. Leonard of Port Maurice

The Hidden Treasure

THE HIDDEN TREASURE:

OR

THE IMMENSE EXCELLENCE

OF

THE HOLY SACRIFICE OF THE MASS;

TOGETHER WITH

A PRACTICAL AND DEVOUT METHOD OF
ASSISTING AT IT WITH FRUIT.

BY

BLESSED LEONARD OF PORT MAURICE.

NEW EDITION,

WITH APPROBATION OF

His Grace the Most Rev. Dr. Cullen,

LORD ARCHBISHOP OF DUBLIN.

DUBLIN:
JAMES DUFFY, 7, WELLINGTON QUAY,
AND
LONDON, 22, PATERNOSTER ROW.
1861.

2, CRAMPTON-QUAY.

The present Work having been revised and examined, We hereby approve it, and recommend it to the Faithful, as well adapted to instruct and edify them.

✠ *PAUL CULLEN,*
ARCHBISHOP OF DUBLIN, AND PRIMATE
OF IRELAND.

Dublin, January, 1861.

CONTENTS.

	Page.
Approbation	ii
Memoir of Blessed Leonard	vii
CHAPTER I.—Three Special Excellences of the august Sacrifice of the Mass	1
CHAPTER II.—A Short and Devout Method of hearing Mass with great Fruit	45
CHAPTER III.—Various Examples to induce all the Faithful of every State and Condition to hear Holy Mass daily	62
§ 1. Examples to induce Priests to offer the Holy Sacrifice of the Mass every Morning, except in case of some legitimate Impediment	64
§ 2. Examples of various Princes, Kings, and Emperors	74
§ 3. Examples for Ladies in high Station	80
§ 4. For Women in general	83
§ 5. For Tradesmen and Artisans	87
§ 6. For Servants and Farm Labourers	94
§ 7. An awful Warning to all those who do not set proper Value on the great Treasure of the Holy Mass	98

An Easy Method of assisting at Holy Mass with great Fruit	107—112
Exercises of Preparation and Thanksgiving for Confession and Holy Communion	113
Prayers before Confession	ib.
Another Prayer	116
Prayer after Confession	ib.
Prayers before Holy Communion	117
Act of Faith	ib.
Act of Adoration	118

CONTENTS.

	Page.
Act of Hope	119
Act of Love	ib.
Act of Contrition	121
Act of Humility	122
An Act of Desire	124
An Act of Offering	125
Devout Exercises after Communion	ib.
Act of Thanksgiving	127
Act of Petition	129
Act of Oblation	131
Act of Self-Oblation to be made every Morning	ib.
How you should act after receiving the Holy Communion	133
The Viaticum	ib.
Conduct in the Church	ib.

PREFACE.

In presenting to the pious reader this new edition of the "Hidden Treasure," the Editor would fain hope that it will obtain a favourable reception from all those who desire to strengthen their souls with holy and wholesome truths, supplied from the sacred Scriptures and other sources recognized by the Church. The golden simplicity and unction which characterize the writings of the Blessed Leonard of Port Maurice, are their strongest recommendation to all classes of Catholics, and we need only refer to the experience of the pious missionaries who constantly exhort the faithful to study the pages of the "Hidden Treasure," for incontestible proofs of the numerous and singular blessings which have resulted from such reading. The holy author of this edifying little volume was born in the town of Port Maurice, not far from Genoa, in the year 1676, and received in baptism the name of Paul Jerome. When twelve years old he was confided by his parents to an uncle residing at Rome, who committed him to the care of the illustrious Fathers of the Society of Jesus, from whom he received his first lessons in sacred and profane literature. Having made wonderful proficiency in his studies, under the guidance of such eminent teachers, and given indubitable signs that he was destined by God to achieve great works for his honour and glory, Paul Jerome resolved to abandon the world for the austerities of a religious life, and he accordingly sought and obtained admission into the convent of St. Bonaventure—one of the Franciscan monasteries at Rome—when he had completed his twenty-second year. Thenceforth the life of this blessed servant of God was an uninterrupted series of truly apostolical labours in Tuscany and throughout the Pontifical States; so much so, indeed, that on completing his fifty-third year, he could count one hundred and three missions which he had given to enormous multitudes, who justly regarded him as a special instrument in the hands of Almighty God. Notwithstanding his excessive labours in the Lord's vineyard, extending over a period of forty-five years, Blessed Leonard lived to the age of seventy-five, when, after a short and painless illness, he surrendered his soul to God on the 26th November, 1751. The Editor deems it superfluous to add another word to the little he has already said, regarding the merits of this admirable work, since those, whose judgment may not be doubted, have pronounced it to be a key with which the pious Christian can unlock the treasury of heaven, and thus draw largely on its all-sanctifying riches.

THE HIDDEN TREASURE,
&c. &c.

CHAPTER I.

THREE SPECIAL EXCELLENCES OF THE AUGUST SACRIFICE OF THE MASS.

I. How it outrages one's patience to be obliged to listen to the insulting language of certain libertines, who, from time to time, utter scandalous propositions, which savour of atheism, and are the very bane of true piety. "*A Mass more or a Mass the less,*" say those impious people, "*counts for nothing. It is a hardship to be obliged to assist at Mass on holidays. The Mass of such a Priest is as long as that of the Holy Week, and I always hurry out of the church when I see him approaching the altar.*" The person who speaks in this manner shows unmistakeably that he has little or no respect for the most holy sacrifice of the Mass. Have you considered what the holy sacrifice of the Mass really is? It is the sun of Christianity, the soul of Faith, the centre of the Catholic religion, the grand object of all her rites, ceremonies, and Sacraments; in a word, it is the condensation of all that is good and beautiful in the Church of God. Now, let me beseech you who read these pages, to ponder well on what I am about to say to you in the following instruction.

II. It is an undeniable truth, that all the religions that existed ever since the foundation of the world, have always had some sacrifice as an essential part of the worship which they offered to God. But as their laws were either vain or imperfect, so likewise were their sacrifices either vain or imperfect. Vainest of all vain things were the sacrifices of the idolaters, nor is it necessary, at any length, to dwell on this subject; and imperfect, too, were the sacrifices of the Jews, notwithstanding that they once professed the true religion, for their sacrifices were shadowy and defective, so much so that St. Paul* designates them "weak and poor elements," because they were incapable of cancelling sin or conferring grace. The one great sacrifice of our holy religion, that is the Mass, is holy, perfect, and in every respect complete, for by it the faithful render the highest honor to God, professing, at the same time, their own nothingness, and the supreme dominion which God has over all. David† called this sacrifice the "*Sacrifice of Justice,*" and truly, indeed, because it contains the Just of the Just, the Holy of Holies, nay, Justice and Sanctity itself, and because it sanctifies souls by the infusion of grace, and the rich outpouring of the gifts which it bestows. As it is, therefore, a sacrifice so holy, so venerable, nay, and transcendently excelling all others, we will now unfold briefly, yet succinctly, some of its divine excellences, in order that you may be enabled to form a proper notion of this great treasure. I say some of them, be-

* Gal. iv. 9.   † Ps. iv. 6.

cause to enumerate them all would be to undertake what is far beyond our poor ability.

III. In what does the chief excellence of the Mass consist? In this, namely, that it is essentially the same, nay the very same sacrifice that was offered on the cross of Calvary, with this sole difference, however, that the sacrifice of the cross was bloody, and was offered once, and did, on that one tremendous moment, satisfy fully for all the sins of the world; while the sacrifice of the altar is an unbloody sacrifice, which can be repeated throughout all times, and was instituted in order to apply to each of us that universal atonement which Christ made for us on Calvary. In a word, the bloody sacrifice was the instrument of our redemption, and the unbloody places us in possession of it. The one opened to us the treasury of the merits of Christ our Lord, and the other gives us the use of that never-failing treasury. Remember well, however, that in the Mass there is made, *not* a mere representation, nor a simple commemoration of the passion and death of the Redeemer, but in a certain sense in it there is performed that very same most holy action that was performed on Calvary; and it can be said with entire truth, that in every Mass our Redeemer returns to die mystically for us, although He does not die really, thus being at one and the same time alive, and, as it were, slain, according to the passage of the Apocalypse, "I saw a lamb standing, as it were slain." On Christmas Day the Church represents the birth of our Lord, but it is not true that our Lord is born on that day. On the Feast of the Ascension, and on that of Pentecost, the Church commemorates the ascent of our Lord to heaven, and the coming down of the Holy Spirit to men on earth, but it is not true that the Lord ascends on that day to heaven, or that the Holy Spirit descends visibly to earth. But the same cannot be said of the mystery of the Holy Mass, because in it there is made no simple representation, but, on the contrary, the very same sacrifice, in an unbloody manner, that was once offered on the cross with the effusion of blood; that very same body, that very same blood, that very same Jesus that was once offered on Calvary, is now offered in the holy Mass. "The work of our redemption," says the Church, "is carried on"—ah, verily it is carried on in the Mass, and therein is repeated the same sacrifice that was offered on the cross. Oh, the stupendous work! Now answer me candidly, when you are going to the church to hear Mass, do you bear in mind that you are going to Calvary to be present at the Redeemer's death? If this thought was deep in your soul, would you venture into the holy place with unbecoming gait, or in apparel that is immodest? Had Magdalene gone to the foot of the cross on Calvary, bedizened, perfumed, and with a display of finery such as she wore in the time of her sinfulness, what would have been said of her? Now what are we to say of you who go to the holy place dressed out as for some merry-making? What should be said of you if you were to profane that most august sacrifice by unbeseeming conduct, such as nods, salutations, laughter, whisperings, or, worse than all, lascivious and sacrilegious glancings? Iniquity is abominable on all occasions and in all places, but the sins that are committed during Mass, and under the shadow of the altar, are sins which call down God's signal maledictions, " Cursed be he who doeth the work of the Lord deceitfully."* Ponder seriously now while I unfold to you other and still more marvellous excellences of this most precious treasure.

IV. It would seem that the holy sacrifice of the Mass could not have a more august prerogative than this—namely, that it is no mere copy, but original with the sacrifice of the cross. Its perfection is brought out by considering that, like the sacrifice of the cross, it has a God-man for its priest. Certain it is, that in presence of so holy a sacrifice three things should always be borne in mind: the priest who offers, the victim offered, and the majesty of God, to whom the oblation is made. Now, ponder well on the indescribable glory of the holy Sacrifice, and let each of these three considerations sink deeply into your soul. The priest who offers it is God made-man—Christ Jesus; the victim is the life of God; nor is it offered to any other than God. Revive your faith, therefore, and recognise in that priest, who makes the offering, the adorable person of our Lord Jesus Christ. He is the *primary* offerer, not only because He has instituted this holy Sacrifice, and given it all efficacy through His merits, but also because in every Mass He, Himself, for love of us, deigns to transubstantiate the bread and the wine

* Jer. xlviii. 10.

into his most holy body and into his most precious blood. Behold, then, the grandest prerogative of the holy Mass—its priest is God made-man; and when you see the celebrant at the altar, remember that his grandest dignity consists in being the minister of this invisible and eternal priest, our divine Redeemer himself. Hence it follows that the sacrifice must be grateful to God, although the priest who celebrates might happen to be iniquitous and sacrilegious, since the primary offerer is Christ our Lord, and the priest is merely His simple minister. Thus, for example, the person who gives alms through the hands of a servant is justly termed the primary donor; and although the servant may be a wicked and sinful person, provided the giver be good and virtuous, the alms cannot fail to have their reward. Blessed, therefore, be God, who has given us a holy, nay a most holy priest, who, not only in every place (the Christian religion being now propagated to the ends of the world), but at all times, every day and every hour (for the sun rises for others whilst it sets to us), offers to the eternal Father this divine sacrifice. Therefore, at all hours, and in every quarter of the globe, this most holy priest offers to the Father his soul and his entire self for us; and this He does as often as there are Masses celebrated throughout the entire universe. Oh, immense treasure! Oh, mine of exhaustless wealth that we possess in the Church of God! Oh, happy we, could we but assist at all those Masses! What a capital of merits might we not then lay up! what an accumulation of graces in this life, and what a fund of glory in the world to come would not that devout assistance provide for us!

V. But why do I use the word *assistance?* Surely those who hear Mass not only perform the function of assisting, but they are likewise offerers, nay, and have a right to be called priests, according to the Apocalypse,* " Thou hast made us to our God a kingdom, and priests;" for, indeed, the celebrating priest is a public minister of the Church in common, and at the same time, a mediator for all the faithful, and particularly for those who assist at Mass with the invisible priest, who is Christ; and together with him he offers to the eternal Father, in behalf of all and of himself, the great price of human redemption. But he is not alone in this most august function, since all those who assist at Mass concur with him in offering the holy sacrifice; and it is on this account that the priest turns to the people and says, " Pray, brethren, that mine and *your* sacrifice may be acceptable," in order that we may understand that although he performs the part of principal minister, all those who are present make the great offering along with him. Hence, when you assist at Mass you perform to a certain extent the part of a priest. What say you now? Will you ever again dare to hear Mass sitting, whispering, looking idly about you, nay, sometimes even sleeping; contenting yourselves with reciting, thoughtlessly it may be, a few vocal prayers, heedless, entirely heedless of the tremendous office of priest which you are exercising. Alas! I cannot refrain from exclaim-

---

* Apoc. v. 10.

ing: Oh, stupid world, that does not estimate mysteries so sublime! How is it possible that any one can remain in presence of the altar with a distracted mind and a dissipated heart at a moment when the angels hover there trembling and astonished, absorbed in contemplating the effects of such a stupendous work?

VI. Are you astonished at hearing me call the Mass a stupendous work? if so, let me ask you what can there be more stupendous than the effect produced by a few words pronounced by a simple priest? In fact, what tongue is there—angelic or human—that can adequately describe a power so measureless? who could ever have imagined that the tongue of a man, which of itself has not power to lift a straw from the ground, would have been endowed by divine grace with a power—oh, how stupendous!—that can cause the Son of God to descend from heaven on earth? This power far excels that of being able to remove mountains, drain seas dry, or regulate the motions of the planets; nay more, the possession of this power, to a certain extent, rivals that first *fiat* by which God created all things out of nothing, and in a certain sense it seems to excel that other *fiat* by which the great Virgin attracted the Eternal Word to her bosom: for she did nothing more than supply matter for Christ's body which was formed from her most pure blood, but not by herself, that is not by her own act. But entirely different, and wonderful beyond describing, is the sacramental manner in which the words of the priest, whom Christ employs as his instrument, reproduce Him every time that he consecrates. Blessed John Buono, of Mantua, gave a singular illustration of this truth to a friend of his, a hermit, who was not able to comprehend how the words of a priest could be endowed with such a tremendous power as to be capable of changing the substance of bread into the body of Jesus Christ, and the substance of wine into his blood. Let me add, moreover, that this poor hermit unhappily consented to doubts which the devil suggested. The good servant of God, perceiving the man's error, brought him to a fountain from which he took a vessel of water and gave it to him to drink. After he had drunk he protested that he never before, at any period of his life, had tasted such a delicious wine. Hearing this, Blessed John Buono said to him, "Dear brother, does not this convince you of the marvellous truth? If God has been pleased to change the water into wine through the agency of such a creature as I am, how much the more readily should you believe that by virtue of the words pronounced by the priest, which are the words of God, the bread and the wine are converted into the substance of the body and blood of Christ? And who shall presume to limit God's omnipotence?" This singular illustration, and the words of Blessed John, dissipated every doubt from the mind of the hermit, who afterwards did great penance for his sin. A little faith, but a lively faith, will convince us that the ineffable excellences contained in this adorable sacrifice are beyond counting; nor will we be surprised at seeing the miracle repeated over and over again at every hour and in every place, since the sacred humanity of Jesus Christ is endowed with a kind, if we may so speak, of immensity not granted to other bodies. This multiplied existence of our Lord in the Sacrament was, as we are told, illustrated to an unbelieving Jew by an illiterate woman. The Jew was standing in the public street, where there was a great crowd, and among them the woman, at the very moment when a priest, carrying the holy viaticum to a sick person, made his appearance, followed by a large multitude. All the people knelt to adore the holy viaticum as it was borne along; but the Jew stirred not, nor did he offer any sign of reverence. Perceiving this, the woman, roused to indignation, arose, pulled the cap off the Jew's head and gave him a cuff on the cheek, exclaiming at the same time, "Infidel! why do you not adore the true God in the divine Sacrament?" "What true God?" said the Jew. "If the true God were there it would follow that there must be an infinity of Gods, since you assert that there is one on each of your altars any time that Mass is celebrated." Hearing this, the woman took a sieve, and placing it between the Jew's eyes and the sun, told him to look at the sun's rays through the apertures of this sieve. When he had done as she directed, she continued, "Tell me now, Jew, are there many suns, or only one, passing through the apertures of this sieve?" to which the Jew answered, "There is only one sun." "Then," replied the woman, "why do you wonder if God, made-man and shrouded in the Sacrament, though one, indivisible, and unchanged, should, through excess of love for us, present Himself *really* and *truly* on different altars?" This was amply sufficient to convince the Jew; so much so, that he was compelled to acknowledge the truth of our holy faith. Oh, holy faith! a single ray of thy light is sufficient to enable the most illiterate to answer with fervor of spirit. Oh, who will dare to set limits to God's omnipotence? So profoundly was St. Teresa impressed with the idea of that omnipotence, that she was accustomed to say, "the sublimer, deeper, and more abstruse the mysteries of our holy faith, the firmer and devouter is my belief, and the greater is my reverence for them." And, indeed, she was justified in expressing herself thus, for she was thoroughly convinced that the omnipotence of God can effect still greater wonders far above our feeble intelligence. Revive your faith, therefore, and acknowledge that this divine sacrifice is the miracle of miracles, the wonder of wonders, and that its highest excellence consists in its being incomprehensible to our limited understanding. Amazed at such marvellous goodness of our God, never cease repeating, Oh, treasure inestimable! oh, treasure beyond all human comprehension! But lest its prodigious excellence should not awaken these sentiments in your soul, let the necessity of such a holy sacrifice inspire them.

VII. If there were no sun in the heavens what would be the condition of this world? Alas! all would be darkness, sterility, and indescribable misery. And if we had not the holy Mass what would become of us? Oh, wretched indeed would our condition be, deprived of every good, overwhelmed with every evil; for we should then be, as it were, a target for the thunderbolt of God's anger. Some there are who seem astonished when they fancy that our good God has, in a certain sense, changed His mode of governing the world since the ancient times; for, in the latter He was wont to be called the God of armies, and He used to speak to the people out of the clouds with bolts of thunder in His hands; for, indeed, He punished crime with all the rigor of His justice. For one single adultery He put five-and-twenty thousand of the tribe of Benjamin to the sword. For an act of vainglory committed by David in making a census of his kingdom, He sent a terrible plague, which in a very short time swept off seventy thousand of the population. For one irreverent and incautious glance He slew fifty thousand of the Betsamites. And in these our times He tolerates not only vanities and frivolities, but adulteries the most sordid, scandals the most barefaced, nay, and the most frightful blasphemies which many Christians cast on His most holy Name. How then do we account for all this? Why this difference in His mode of governing? Is it because our ingratitudes are more excusable than those of our predecessors? Quite the contrary, indeed; for as we have received blessings far surpassing those that were conferred on the Jews in the old dispensation, so are we far more culpable than they. The holy sacrifice of the Mass is the true and sole reason of such stupendous clemency, for in it we offer to the eternal Father the great victim, Jesus Christ. This is the sun of our holy Church which dissipates the clouds and restores serenity to the heavens. This, indeed, is the celestial rainbow that stills the tempest of divine justice. For my own part, I am persuaded that if it were not for the holy Mass the world would have long since tottered from its foundations, crushed beneath the enormous weight of so many accumulated iniquities. The Mass is the ponderous and powerful supporter on which the world rests—which keeps it from falling into horrid chaos. Will not this reflection convince you of the necessity of this divine sacrifice? But as this alone is not enough we must know how to turn to good account the blessings which it holds out to us. Wherefore, when assisting at the holy sacrifice, let us bear in mind a memorable fact recorded in the life of Alfonso Albuquerque, who, with his fleet, being overtaken by a terrible storm at sea which threatened him with certain death, had recourse to the following expedient: taking a tender child that was at that moment aboard his ship, and holding him up to heaven he exclaimed, "If we are sinners, this innocent babe surely is free from sin. O Lord! for the sake of this sinless child save us, sinners, from death." Would you believe it? God was so appeased by the sight of that pure infant that the storm was stilled, and the horror of impending death, which caused the sailors to weep and tremble, was turned into transports of joy. Now, what think you does the eternal Father when the priest, elevating the most holy victim of the altar exhibits to Him the innocence of His divine Son ? Ah, surely His tender compassion cannot but be moved at sight of the immaculate innocence of Jesus, and surely that divine compassion must, in a certain sense, be constrained to still the fierce storms that assail us, nay, and to provide for our necessities. Ah, indeed, if it were not for this most holy victim, once offered for us on the cross, and now daily offered on our altars, we one and all might renounce all hope of heaven and look on hell as our final destination. Yes, assuredly, were it not for this ever blessed victim hell, hell should be our portion! But this treasure of the holy Mass revives our hopes, and encourages us to look for everlasting glory in that paradise which cannot be forfeited except by our own folly and sinfulness. If, therefore, it is the duty of a Christian to twine his heart's affections round our altars, and to perfume them with incense and flowers of sweetest odour, it is still more necessary to honor them with purity and modesty, since they are, in fact, the *mercy-seat* from which we derive all good. With joined hands, therefore, and hearts thrilling with holy love, let us thank the eternal Father who has so mercifully obliged us to offer to Him this heavenly victim; but let us be still more thankful for the countless benefits we can draw from it, provided we make the offering in the spirit of true believers, and for the sublime ends for which He has bestowed this precious treasure upon us.

VIII. A proper appreciation of what is high-minded and honorable must assuredly act with great power on the human heart; but a sense of what tends to our own individual advantage not only stimulates our efforts, but eventually enables us to achieve a triumph, no matter how great may be the obstacles thrown in our way. If, therefore, you set little value on the excellence and necessity of the holy Mass, how can you form any idea of the vast benefits that it bestows on the living and the dead, on the just man and the sinner, in life and death, nay, and even after death itself? Imagine yourself to be the debtor described in the Gospel, who, overwhelmed by the weighty amount of ten thousand talents which he owed, and being commanded to pay, excused himself, and supplicated piteously for time to discharge his obligation, " Have patience with me and I will pay thee all;"* and the self-same thing should you do, who owe not only one but many sums to the bank of divine justice. You ought to humble yourself and beg time, even as much as is sufficient to hear Mass, and you may rest satisfied that you will thus be enabled to discharge all your debts without drawback or abatement. The Angelic Doctor, St. Thomas, teaches us what are the debts that we owe to God, and he says that they are four, and that each of them is infinite.

The first is to praise and honor the infinite majesty of God, which is eminently worthy of infinite honor and infinite praise.

The second is to make satisfaction for all the sins we have committed.

The third is to thank and bless God for all the benefits He has bestowed on us.

* Matt. xviii. 26.

The fourth is to supplicate Him constantly, as the giver of all good gifts.

How then can we, miserable creatures, who depend on God for the very air we breathe, make any satisfaction for debts so numerous or so weighty ? Let me at once, therefore, point out to you the easiest way of doing so, and let me add that this way of satisfying divine justice is one which should console me, you, and all of us. Let us be diligent in hearing Mass as often as possible, and with all possible devotion ; and furthermore, let us endeavour to have as many Masses as possible celebrated for our intention. By this means, be our debts weighty as they may, and countless beyond numbering, there can be no doubt that we will be able to discharge them all completely and entirely by the treasure which is derivable from the holy Mass. And in order that you may be fully enlightened, and have a perfect knowledge of each of these debts, I will now explain them all one by one, for your edification ; and here let me remark, that this mode of proceeding must afford you the greatest consolation, since it makes known to you the great practical advantages, and the inexhaustible wealth that you can draw from so rich a mine on all occasions, and in all our necessities.

IX. The first debt by which we have bound ourselves to God is to render Him supreme honor. Even the natural law lays down this as an indispensable obligation, namely, that every inferior owes homage to his superior, and the more exalted the latter, the greater the homage to which he is entitled. Hence it follows, that as God possesses infinite greatness, we are bound to return Him love, so to say, infinitely infinite. But, alas! where will we, miserable creatures, find any offering worthy of our Creator? Pass in review before your eyes all the creatures of this world, and you will not find one of them worthy of God. Ah, what offering can there be worthy of God except God Himself? And He who is seated on the throne of His immensity vouchsafes to descend and offer Himself as a victim on our altars, in order that our homage may correspond perfectly with the pre-eminence of His infinite majesty. And this is effected in the holy Mass, in which God is honored as he deserves to be honored, because He is honored by God Himself, that is by Jesus, who, placing Himself a victim on our altars, adores the most holy Trinity by an act of indescribable submission, such as no other can offer; so much so that all the offerings of all created beings, compared to this humiliation of our Divine Redeemer, are as the feeble light of the stars before the meridian splendours of the sun. 'Tis related of a holy woman, whose soul was intensely inflamed with love of God, that she was accustomed to express her ardent longings thus: "Ah, my God, my God, I wish that I had as many hearts and tongues as there are leaves on the trees, atoms in the air, and drops of water in the sea, to love thee as Thou deservest to be loved! Oh, that I could encircle all earth's creatures with my hands, and lay them at thy feet, in order that they might be inflamed with love of Thee, provided I might love Thee more intensely than them all, nay, more intensely than all the angels and saints, more than Paradise itself!" One day, when she was thus breathing forth these devout longings with redoubled fervour, she had the happiness to hear our Lord answering her in these words: "Dear daughter, be consoled, because, by a single Mass at which you assist devoutly, you can render to me all that glory for which your heart is on fire, nay, and infinitely more." And are you astounded at hearing this assertion? But you have no reason to be so; because as our good Jesus is not only man, but true and omnipotent God, He, by humbling Himself upon the altar, renders, by that very act of humiliation, infinite homage and infinite honor to the most holy Trinity, so that we who co-operate with Him in offering the great sacrifice are thus enabled, through him, to offer unto God homage and honor which is infinite. Oh, stupendous fact! Let us repeat it over and over again, since it never can be too deeply graven on our memories, "Certainly, certainly, by hearing holy Mass with proper dispositions, we offer unto our God homage and honor that is infinite!" Here, now, let holy amazement overwhelm your souls, and reflect that nothing can be truer than the proposition already laid down, namely, that by assisting devoutly at holy Mass, we bestow on God honor far surpassing that which all the choirs of angels and saints, aggregated into one great whole, can bestow upon Him in heaven, for, notwithstanding their state of blessedness, they, like ourselves, are mere creatures, and thus their homage is limited and finite; whereas, in the

Mass, Jesus humbles Himself, a humiliation which is infinite in value and merits, and consequently the homage and honor which we render to God, through Him, in the Mass, is a homage and honor that is infinite. And since this grand truth cannot be doubted, ought we not congratulate ourselves on having it in our power to be able to satisfy this first debt by hearing the holy Mass? Oh, blind world, when wilt thou open thine eyes to a truth so grand and so important? And yet, alas! you will have the folly to say, "*a Mass the more or a Mass the less*" counts for nothing! Oh, abominable blindness!

X. Our second debt or obligation to God is to satisfy His justice for the numerous and enormous sins which we have committed. Oh, what a mighty debt this is! A single mortal sin so preponderates in the scale of divine justice, that all the good works of all the martyrs and saints who have been, are, or ever shall be, could not satisfy for it; and yet, by means of the holy Mass, if we but consider its intrinsic value and holiness, we are enabled to make complete satisfaction for all the sins we have committed. But in order that you may rightly comprehend how deeply you are indebted to Jesus, weigh well what I am about to say to you. Although He has been offended and outraged by our sins, yet, not content with having satisfied divine justice for us on Calvary, He has given, and continually does give us, the self-same means of satisfying it (divine justice) in the holy sacrifice of the Mass, because, by renewing in the Mass that offering which Jesus made to the eternal

Father on the cross, for the sins of the whole world, that very same divine blood, which He once poured out to ransom the human race, comes now to be applied to each and every one of us, because it is specially offered in the Mass for the sins of him who celebrates, and also for the sins of all those who assist at so tremendous a sacrifice. Let me not be understood as saying, that the sacrifice of the Mass cancels our sins *immediately* by itself, as the Sacrament of Penance does, but, rather, that it cancels them *mediately*, by obtaining for us various most necessary aids, such as interior impulses, holy inspirations, and actual graces, all of which are calculated to enable us to do true penance for our sins, either during the time of Mass or at some other opportune period. And it is for this reason that none but God can tell how many souls arise from the slough and chains of sin by means of the extraordinary aids which they derive from this divine sacrifice. And here let me impress on you, that although the sacrifice of the Mass cannot avail him who is in mortal sin as *propitiatory*, it, nevertheless, can avail him as *supplicatory*, so that all sinners ought to hear many Masses, in order that they may obtain more easily the grace of conversion. To souls, however, that live in grace, it gives wonderful strength, calculated to maintain them in the state of grace; and it likewise cancels, by itself (according to the more generally received opinion), all venial sins, always provided that we have repented of them in the aggregate, according to what St. Augustine has left on record:

"Whoever hears Mass devoutly will receive great strength to avoid the commission of mortal sin, and he shall likewise obtain remission of all the venial sins that he may have committed up to that time." Nor should this astonish you, if you bear in mind what St. Gregory relates of a poor woman who caused Mass to be celebrated every Monday for the soul of her husband, who had been made prisoner by certain barbarians, and who, she thought, was dead; for the holy sacrifice caused the chains to fall from his feet, and the handcuffs from his wrists, so that during the whole time these Masses were being celebrated he was free, as he avowed when he came back to her. How much the more should we believe that a sacrifice so tremendous and holy must be most efficacious in releasing us from the spiritual chains, namely, venial sins, which keep the soul, as it were, imprisoned, and prevent it from acting with that liberty and fervour with which it would have acted if it were not for such impediments? Oh, thrice holy Mass, which ennobles us with the liberty of the sons of God, and satisfies for all the penalties which our sins deserve.

XI. But you will say to me: "Therefore, it is quite enough for us to assist at, or cause a single Mass to be celebrated, in order to get rid of all those most weighty debts we owe to God by reason of the many sins we have committed, because the Mass being of infinite value we can thereby render to God an infinite satisfaction." Do not rush to so rash a conclusion, I beseech you, for although the Mass is of infinite value, you must know, nevertheless, that God accepts it in a manner limited and finite, and conformably to the greater or less perfection in the dispositions of him who celebrates, causes to be celebrated, or assists at the sacrifice. "*Whose faith and devotion are known unto Thee,*" says the Church in the canon of the Mass, thus teaching us, by this manner of expression, what the great divines inculcate, namely, that the greater or less satisfaction applied by the sacrifice in our behalf, is determined by the greater or less perfection in the dispositions of him who celebrates, causes to be celebrated, or assists at the sacrifice, as we have said before. Now, only think of the folly of those who go in search of a Mass celebrated rapidly, or, what is worse, who assist thereat with little or no devotion; think of the culpable indifference of those who never ask to have Mass celebrated for them, and who are careless in selecting for that purpose priests who are most remarkable for their fervour and devotion. "It is certain," says St. Thomas, "that all sacrifices, *as sacraments*, are equal in dignity, but they are not equal, however, as far as regards the effects that flow from them; hence, the greater the actual or habitual piety of the celebrant, the greater shall also be the fruit of the application of the holy sacrifice, so that to make no distinction between a tepid and a devout priest in the function of celebrant, is to be indifferent whether the net with which you would fish be big or little. All this is equally applicable to those who assist at Mass. And although I would exhort you with all my energies to hear as many Masses as you can, yet I feel bound to admonish you that you should have more regard for the *greater devotion* than for the greater number, because if your devotion at one single Mass be greater than that of a man who assists at fifty, you will give more honor to God in that single one, and you will derive more benefit from it, than the other does from fifty. "In satisfaction," says St. Thomas, "*the disposition of the party offering is more regarded than the quantity of the oblation;*" and although it is certain (as a profound authority lays down), that in some particular instance the justice of God might be satisfied for all the sins of the most heinous criminal through one Mass heard with entire and unalloyed devotion, according to the Council of Trent, which teaches that in consideration of the offering made in this holy sacrifice, God grants the gift of penitence, and then through the instrumentality of true penitence, pardons the most grievous, enormous, nay, and sins of infinite magnitude; nevertheless, since neither the internal disposition with which you assist at Mass is manifest to yourself, nor the satisfaction corresponding to it, you ought to secure yourselves as much as you possibly can by hearing many Masses, and hearing them with all possible devotion. And thrice happy will you be if you cherish great confidence in the mercy of God, that operates so wonderfully in this divine sacrifice; thrice happy, indeed, if you assist as frequently as possible at Mass with lively faith and devout recollection in your heart. Acting thus you may reasonably cherish the hope of going direct to heaven without touching even the confines of Purgatory. To Mass, therefore, to Mass, and never let such a scandalous proposition as "a Mass more or a Mass less counts for nothing," be heard from your lips.

XII. Our third debt is one of gratitude for the countless benefits that our most loving God has bestowed upon us. Contemplate in one accumulation all the gifts and all the graces which you have received from God; so many gifts of nature and grace, body, soul, and senses, intellectual faculties, health, and life itself; add to all these the very life of His Son Jesus, and the death that He suffered for love of us; and then say to yourself, does not all this increase a thousand fold the debt that I owe to God? But when will we ever be able to thank Him as we ought? If the law of gratitude is observed by even the untamed beasts that have often changed their fierce nature into gentleness to those from whom they received a kindness, much more, surely, should it be observed by men gifted with the great powers of reason, and so eminently endowed by the divine liberality. But then, again, so great is our poverty that we have no means of making a return for the least of the countless blessings which we have received from God; because as the very least of them all comes to us from the hands of a Majesty so exalted, and accompanied by infinite charity, it acquires an infinite value and obligates us to an infinite correspondence.

Oh, wretched we! if we cannot sustain the weight of one single benefit how will we be able to bear the still greater weight of benefits so great, nay, and so innumerable? Are we then placed in the direful necessity of living and dying ingrates to our supreme benefactor? No, no! take heart and be of good cheer, for the manner of thanking our good God completely was taught us by holy David, who, beholding with prophetic eyes this divine sacrifice, clearly confesses that nothing save the holy Mass can render due thanks to God. "What shall I render unto the Lord for all His benefits to me?" asks the psalmist; and then answering himself he continues: "I will take the cup of salvation," (according to another version) "I will raise on high the chalice of the Lord,"—that is, I will offer a sacrifice most acceptable to Him, and with this alone I shall satisfy the debt of so many and so singular blessings. Bear in mind, likewise, that this sacrifice was instituted principally by our Redeemer for this end, namely—to acknowledge the divine beneficence and to thank it; and it is on this account that it is emphatically called *Eucharist*, which signifies an *offering of thanks*. It was He Himself who gave us the example, when at the Last Supper, before consecrating in that first Mass, He raised His eyes to heaven and thanked His heavenly Father. Oh, divine thanksgiving, that discovers to us the sublime end for which this tremendous sacrifice was instituted; and invites us to conform ourselves to our supreme Head, in order that in every Mass at which we assist we may know how to avail ourselves of so great a treasure by offering it in gratitude to our supreme Benefactor. And that we may be more zealous in carrying out the divine intentions, let us always remember that all Paradise, the Virgin Mother and the angels and saints, exult when we offer this tribute of thanks to so great a Monarch.

XIII. It is related of the venerable sister Francesca Farnese, that her whole life was tormented by a thousand yearnings of love, because she felt that she knew not how to return adequate thanks to her Lord for the divine blessings with which He had covered her from head to foot. It was on one of those occasions, when she was lamenting her inability to offer to God the gratitude which He so eminently deserved, that the Virgin Mother appeared to her, and placed the heavenly Infant in her arms, saying, " Take Him, for He is yours, and with Him alone you will find it easy to discharge all your obligations." Oh, thrice blessed Mass, which places the Son of God not only in our arms and hands but also in our hearts! " A little child has been given to us,"* in order that we may be enabled to do that which exceeds our unassisted weakness; for most certainly with His aid we will be able to discharge, fully and entirely, the debt of gratitude that we owe to God. Nay, in the holy Mass we give to God, in a particular sense, something more than what He hath bestowed upon us; if not in reality, at all events in appearance; since once only the eternal Father has given us His divine Son in the incarnation,

---

* Isaiah, ix. 6.

and we give Him back to Him again countless times in this holy sacrifice. Hence, to a certain extent, it seems that we possess the advantage, not, indeed, in the quality of the gift, since nothing greater than the Son of God could have been given to us, but apparently by returning to Him so often and repeatedly the very identical gift. Oh, great and most loving God, would that each of us had countless tongues to return thee infinite thanks for this inestimable treasure of the holy Mass with which thou hast enriched us! Have you as yet learned to set due value on this great treasure? Ah, if hitherto it has lain a treasure *hidden* from you, now that you have begun to know its transcendent value, let a holy amazement overwhelm you, and repeat, over and over again, incessantly: Oh, treasure incomparable! oh, treasure beyond all price!

XIV. But the infinite benefit of the holy Mass does not end here; for it enables us, moreover, to pay the fourth debt which we owe to God. I have already told you that that debt is one which obliges you to supplicate Him incessantly, and to ask new graces of Him. You are well aware that your necessities of soul and body are grievous and numerous; and you know, besides, that you must needs have recourse to Him at every moment of your existence for His compassionating help, since He, and He alone, is the chief source of all our good, temporal as well as eternal. But, on the other hand, with what dispositions of heart or soul can you supplicate Him to give you additional aids of grace, seeing, as you do, the limitless ingratitude you have exhibited to Him, notwithstanding the countless graces bestowed upon you? Nay, have you not turned the very graces He gave you into so many insults and outrages against Him? Nevertheless, let not your heart wax faint, but rather be of good hope; because, if you have not deserved those graces our good Jesus has deserved them for you. In fact, for this end He has deigned to become in the Mass a pacifying Victim, that is, a supplicating sacrifice, in order to obtain through it (the Mass), from the eternal Father, all things we may require. Yes, yes, in the holy Mass our dear and beloved Jesus, who is our great high priest, recommends our humble petition to His Father, nay, prays for us and becomes our advocate. If we only remembered that the Virgin Mother unites her supplications with ours to the eternal Father to obtain the graces which we need, how confident should we be that our prayers will be heard? What confidence, what hope, therefore, should we not cherish when we bear in mind that in the Mass Jesus Himself prays for us, nay, offers His most precious blood to the eternal Father for us, and becomes our advocate? Oh, thrice blessed Mass, thou art the exhaustless mine of all our good.

XV. But we must go deep into this inestimable mine in order to discover the great treasures that it contains. Oh, what priceless jewels of grace. and virtue! Oh, what super-excellent gifts does not the holy Mass obtain for us! In the first place, it obtains for us all the spiritual graces and all the goods needful for the soul; as, for example, true sorrow and repentance for sins, victory over temptations, no matter whence they come, whether from evil associations with bad companions, or from the internal promptings of our own rebellious nature. Yes, the holy Mass obtains for us all those aids of grace which we need in order to be able to arise from the slough of sin, to stand erect, and walk onward in the ways of God. It likewise obtains for us innumerable holy inspirations and internal impulses, which dispose us to shake off tepidity, and stimulate us to work out our salvation with a fervour more ardent, with will more prompt, and intention purer and more meritorious. All these aids are accompanied by an inestimable treasure; and, indeed, they are the most efficacious means of obtaining from God the grace of final perseverance (on which our eternal salvation depends), and also a moral certainty of eternal beatitude in the life to come, so far as that certainty is vouchsafed to man during his mortal pilgrimage. Furthermore, it obtains for us temporal goods, in as far as they are conducive to the salvation of the soul, health of body, abundance, peace, with the exclusion of all the evils that are opposed to it, be they pestilence, earthquakes, wars, famine, persecutions, litigations, domestic hostilities, calumnies, and insults; in a word, it liberates us from all evils and enriches us with all that is good. And to sum all in one short sentence—the holy Mass is the golden key of Paradise; and since the eternal Father has given us this key, what is there of all His unbounded treasures that He can refuse us? " He that spared not even His own Son, but delivered Him up for us all, how hath He not also, with Him, given us all things?"* Hence, you may clearly understand with what good reason a certain holy priest was wont to say when speaking of the holy Mass: "No matter how great the graces I ask of God for myself or others as often as I celebrate Mass, they all are a mere nothing compared to the offering that I make to Him!" He, indeed, reasoned rightly when he said, "All the favors that I ask of God when celebrating holy Mass are created and finite things, whereas the gifts that I offer to Him are increated and infinite; and so, to balance the account equitably, I am the creditor and He is the debtor." Of course, he knew that the gift, and the power of offering the gift, came primarily from God; and, full of this conviction, he asked great graces of God and obtained still greater. And you, how is it that you are not alive to all this? Why do you not ask great gains and graces? I would advise and exhort you to beseech God, as often as you assist at Mass, to make you a great saint. Do you think that I advise you to ask too much? Well, I tell you that it is not too much. Has not our loving Lord and Master told us in His Gospel, that He is ready to bestow the kingdom of heaven on a man in return for a cup of cold water given for love of Him to a disciple? How, therefore, could He refuse us a hundred heavens, did so many exist, in return for the blood of His blessed Son offered to Him in the Mass? Why,

---

Rom. viii.

therefore, would you hesitate to believe that He will bestow upon you every virtue and all the perfections that are required to make you a saint, yea, a great saint in heaven? Oh, blessed Mass! Let your hearts' wishes, therefore, be multiplied a thousand-fold, and ask as much as you will, always bearing in mind, that you are asking of a God who does not impoverish Himself by giving, and, consequently, the more you ask the more will He give you.

XVI. But, have you reflected on this? Besides the blessings we ask of our good God in the holy Mass, He is wont to grant us many others for which we have not asked Him. St. Jerome affirms this as certain: "Assuredly," says the Saint, "the Lord grants all the favours for which we petition Him in the Mass, provided they be suitable to us; and what is far more admirable, He very often grants us that for which we do not petition Him, always provided that we place no obstacles to His holy designs." Hence, the Mass may be justly described as the sun of the human race, shedding its splendors on the good and bad; nor does there exist on this earth a single soul so perverse, who, hearing holy Mass, does not derive some great benefit from it, often without even thinking of it. We have a singular instance of this in a narrative which Saint Antoninus has left on record; 'tis the following: "Two young men of dissolute habits went one day into a forest to amuse themselves, after one of them had assisted at the holy sacrifice of the Mass. Suddenly the sky was overcast with thick clouds, and amid the loud pealing of the thunder, and the flashes of the lightning, they distinctly heard a mysterious voice crying aloud, 'Kill, kill!' when, lo! the youth who had not heard Mass was struck down by the lightning and burnt to ashes. Terrified at this awful spectacle, his companion took to flight, hoping to save his life, when, to his horror, he heard the same voice repeating the word, 'Kill, kill!' Giving himself up for lost, he was every instant expecting the fatal blow, when he heard another voice replying: *I cannot, I cannot, for to-day he heard 'The Word was made flesh,' and the Mass he heard will not suffer me to strike him dead.*" Oh, how often has God shielded you from death, or, at all events, from many and many a terrible danger, for the sake of the holy Mass at which you assisted! St. Gregory the Great assures you of this in his Book of Dialogues. Hear what he says: "It is most indubitably certain, that whosoever hears Mass shall be secured from many and many a danger, both foreseen and unforeseen." And St. Augustine adds: "Whoever hears Mass devoutly shall be preserved from a sudden death, which is the most awful weapon with which divine justice punishes the sinner." "Lo," says the Saint, "here is the wonderful preservative against a sudden death, hear Mass every day, but hear it with all possible devotion." Whosoever bears about him such an invaluable preservative as this may live morally certain that he shall not be overtaken by such a terrible calamity. There is an opinion, attributed by some to Saint Augustine, namely, that a person does not grow older during the time he assists at the celebration of the holy Mass, but, on the contrary, remains all the time in the same essential vigour in which he was at the beginning of the divine offering. I am not disposed to examine whether this be true or not; but I affirm, that although a person assisting at holy Mass grows older, as far as age is concerned, he, nevertheless, does not grow older in sin, because, as Saint Gregory tells us: " A well-disposed man, who hears holy Mass with the due attention, is preserved in the way of rectitude, while grace and merit increase in him, and he is making new acquisitions of virtue, which render him more and more acceptable to God." Nay, more, St. Bernard informs us, that " more is gained by one single Mass (and let us understand him as speaking of its *intrinsic* value) than by distributing all your substance among the poor, or going on pilgrimages to all the most venerable sanctuaries on this globe." Oh, infinite wealth of the holy Mass! Let this truth strike deep root in your heart. By assisting at or celebrating a single Mass, considered in itself and its intrinsic worth, one may become more meritorious in the sight of God than he who, opening the treasury of his hoarded wealth, distributes all that he possesses for the relief of the poor, or goes on a pilgrimage throughout the universe, visiting, with consummate devotion, the sanctuaries of Jerusalem, Rome, Compostella, Loretto, and every other besides. This grand truth is easily deduced from what St. Thomas, the Angelic Doctor, lays down in the following words: " The holy Mass contains all those fruits, all those graces, nay, and all those infinite treasures which the Son of God scattered so abundantly over His Church in the bloody sacrifice of the cross." Now pause awhile, close the book, read no further for the present, but rather count one by one all those particular utilities or advantages of holy Mass. Ponder them well in silence, and then answer me, will you ever again have any difficulty in believing that a single Mass, viewed in its intrinsic worth and value, is of such efficacy that, according to the Doctors of the Church, it might have sufficed to obtain the salvation of the whole human race? Suppose that our Lord Jesus Christ had not suffered at all on Calvary, and that instead of the bloody sacrifice of the cross He had solely instituted the Mass, with express command that this one single Mass should only be celebrated in all the world *once.* Well, then, had God been pleased to act thus, you must know that that one single Mass, celebrated by the humblest priest on earth, would have been most amply sufficient (considered in its intrinsic value, and so far as its own share in the work is concerned) to obtain from God the salvation of all mankind. Yes, yes; one Mass—admitting the case we have supposed—would have been sufficient to obtain the conversion of all the Turks, of all the Schismatics, in fine, of all the infidels, and even of all the bad Christians, closing the gates of hell against all sinners, and delivering from Purgatory all the souls that are being purged there. But, alas! we, miserable and thoughtless beings, by our tepidity, feeble devotion, and the scandalous immodesties which we commit over and over again while assisting at Mass, how much, oh! how much do we narrow its vast circumference, and render its inestimable value inefficacious. Would that I could ascend to the summit of the loftiest mountain and cry aloud, so that the whole world might hear me exclaiming, Foolish, foolish people, what are ye doing? Why will you not hasten to the churches to assist at every Mass celebrated therein? Why won't you imitate those holy angels, who, according to St. John Chrysostom, descend in thousands from the heavens when Mass is being celebrated, and array themselves before our altars, covered with wings of holy awe, tarrying there during the august sacrifice, in order to intercede more efficaciously for us, knowing well that this is the most opportune time and the most propitious occasion that can be for obtaining favors from heaven? Ah! are you not filled with shame and confusion when you call to mind how little value you have hitherto set upon the holy Mass? Will you not blush for having often and often profaned this thrice sanctified oblation? But what shall I say of you, if, unhappily, you are one of those whose rash and impious tongues dare to say, "*a Mass more or less counts for nothing?*"

XVII. And now, before concluding this instruction, let me remind you, that it was not by mere accident I told you before, that a single Mass, as far as itself is concerned, and in the sense of its intrinsic value, is sufficient to clear Purgatory of all the souls that are being purified there, nay, and to send them straight to Paradise; since the Divine Sacrifice is not only beneficial to the souls of the defunct, as propitiatory and satisfactory of their penance, but it also avails them as *supplicatory*, or, in other words, it obtains for them remission of the Purgatorial pains. Hence, the usage of the Church, which not only offers the holy Mass for the souls in Purgatory, but prays in the holy Sacrifice for their liberation; and in order that you may be excited to commiserate those holy souls, excluded for awhile from the Beatific Vision, let me warn you, that the fire in which they are plunged is as devouring a fire, and nowise less dreadfully intense than that of hell. This assertion is made on the authority of St. Gregory the Great, who, in his Dialogues, informs us, that "the flames of Purgatory are, as it were, the instrument of divine justice, operating with such terrible power as to render the agony of the souls detained there intolerable. These pains," continues the Saint, "far exceed all the tribulations, nay, and martyrdoms that can be witnessed, felt, or imagined in this life;" but far more excruciating to them is the *pain of loss*, or in other words, the temporary exclusion from the beatific vision of God, which, according to the Angelic Doctor (St. Thomas), tortures them with an indescribable agony; a fierce and burning thirst to behold the Supreme Good that is denied to their yearnings. Here now enter into your own heart, and weigh well what I am going to say. If it so happened, that you beheld your own father or mother drowning in a pool of water, and if you could save them by merely stretching out your hand, would you not consider yourself bound by the law of charity and of justice to stretch out your hand for their rescue? And how do you act? Aided by the light of faith, you behold many and many a poor soul immersed in the sea of Purgatorial fires, nay, you behold, it may be, the souls of your nearest and dearest kinsfolk so circumstanced, and yet, will you be so heartless as not to bear the trifling inconvenience of assisting devoutly at one Mass for their release, or the alleviation of their agonies? What sort of a heart have you? Surely you cannot doubt, that even a single Mass can bring exceeding great comfort to those poor souls? If (which God forbid) you have any doubt on this subject, let the words of St. Jerome, who deserves your firmest belief, bring conviction to your soul, and awaken in it a holy compassion. Ponder well what this holy Doctor of the Church tells you. "The souls in Purgatory, for whose comfort the *priest offers the holy Sacrifice of the Mass, suffer no torment while Mass is being celebrated.*" Nay more, he adds, that "*at every Mass many souls are liberated from Purgatory, and ascend to Heaven.* Bear in mind also, that this charity or holy compassion for the poor souls in Purgatory will redound to your own good; and, although I might adduce many proofs in confirmation of this truth, I will confine myself to one well authenticated in the Life of St. Peter Damian. This holy servant of God, when a mere stripling, after losing his parents, was taken into the house of his brother, who treated him very cruelly, compelling him to go barefoot, ragged, and subjecting him to every sort of the most squalid poverty. It so happened, that one day he found a trifling coin, I know not of what value. I leave you to imagine whether he rejoiced or not. As for himself, it seemed to him that he had lit upon a treasure. But how was he to spend it? His pitiable condition, so poor, and so cheerless, suggested to him many ways of employing the money which he had found; but after pondering the matter over and over again in his mind, he resolved to give the coin to a priest, as an alms for celebrating Mass for the holy souls in Purgatory. Well, will you believe it? from that day forward his fortune was changed for the better, for he was adopted by another brother of amiable disposition, who took him into his house, treated him as his own child, clothed him comfortably and sent him to school, whence he afterwards came forth that great man and saint, an ornament to the Cardinalitial purple, and one of the most illustrious pillars of the Church. Now, you see how in one single Mass, which this holy personage caused to be celebrated at some trifling inconvenience, all this happiness had its origin. Oh! most holy Mass, that at one and the same time benefits the living and dead. Oh! most holy sacrifice, so replete with blessings for time and for eternity; for you must bear in mind, that the souls in Purgatory are so grateful to their benefactors, that on being admitted into heaven, they become their advocates, never ceasing in their holy petitions till they see them in possession of glory. A singular proof of what I have here laid down is narrated in the history of a woman—a native of Rome—who for many years led a scandalous life, indulging her passions, and corrupting youth. Nevertheless, notwithstanding the infamy of her career, this unfortunate sinner very frequently caused Mass to be celebrated for the souls in Purgatory; and this, indeed, was the only good she ever did. Now, as we may piously believe, it was these souls who interceded so effectually for their benefactress, that she one day was seized with heartfelt sorrow for her sins—sorrow so vehement that she abandoned wickedness, flung herself at the feet of a zealous priest, made a good general confession, and died soon afterwards with such dispositions as left no doubt of her eternal salvation. This grace of conversion and happy death, so truly marvellous, was attributed by many to the virtue of the Masses which she caused to be celebrated for the holy souls in Purgatory. Let us, therefore, cast off tepidity, and be on our guard, lest "publicans and harlots go into the kingdom of God before us."*

XVIII. If, unhappily, you were one of those hard-hearted misers, who not only lack common charity, neglecting to pray for their deceased friends, never assisting at a single Mass offered for the souls in Purgatory, and what is still worse, trampling on every dictate of justice, by refusing to pay the pious legacies bequeathed by

* Matt. xxi. 31.

their predecessors for Masses; or if you were one of those priests who accumulate large sums given for Masses, which they neglect to celebrate; oh! with what earnestness I would say to your face, " Begone, for you are worse than the veriest devils; aye, infinitely worse, since the demons torment none but reprobate souls, whereas you torment the souls of the *elect*. No, there is no confession that can avail you; no absolution for you that is valid; nay, no confessor that can absolve you, if you do not repent sincerely of so tremendous a crime, and if you do not satisfy, to the last farthing, the obligations that you have contracted with the departed. But you will say to me: " Father, I cannot—I have not the means." What! you cannot, forsooth! you have not the means! But you have means to make fashionable display—means to gratify luxurious and voluptuous tastes—means to lavish on rich feastings, in country-houses, balls, merry-makings, sometimes in the public-house, and sometimes in the horrid dens of vice! But to satisfy your obligations to the living, and what is more, to the poor deceased, you have not the means, you cannot! For shame! But I now understand you rightly, and let me tell you that although there is no one on earth to take you to task for this robbery of the dead, you shall, one day, have to square the account with God, at the bar of His judgment. Go on frustrating the intentions of the deceased, appropriating to yourselves their pious bequests, the monies they bequeathed for Masses, but remember that the oracle of the prophet has registered against you a terrible menace of misfortunes, sickness, worldly reverses, appalling calamities, and irreparable ruin of your substance, life, and honour. Yes, so hath God declared, and He will be true to His word. "*They ate the sacrifices of the dead—thus they provoked him to anger.*"* Yes, yes! ruin, disgrace, and woes without remedy shall overtake those who do not satisfy their obligations to the dead! With good reason, therefore, did the fourth Council of Carthage pronounce all those guilty of this crime *excommunicated*, branding them as *murderers of their neighbours;* and let me add, that the Council of Valence declared that they should be expelled from the Church like infidels. And yet, this is by no means the severest punishment that God inflicts on those whose hearts cherish no love for their deceased brethren; ah, no! the full measure of their punishment is reserved for the other world, for St. James declares, that they shall be judged by God with all the rigour of His justice—without a single particle of mercy, because they showed no mercy to the poor departed. "Judgment without mercy to him that hath not done mercy."† Nay, more, God will permit that their successors shall pay them in the same coin; that is, their last wishes shall not be fulfilled, neither shall the Masses, for which they have provided in their wills, be celebrated; or if celebrated, God will not accept them for *their* souls' sake, but will turn them to the relief and release of deserving souls,

* Ps. cv. † St. James, ii. 13.

who, during their mortal term, had pitying and prayerful hearts for their deceased brethren. It is related in the Chronicles of our Order, that one of our friars appeared, after death, to a companion, and showed him the marks of the bitter punishment he had to endure in Purgatory, particularly because he had been negligent in celebrating Masses for his deceased Brothers. He likewise declared, that all that had been done for him up to that moment was of no avail to him, and that the very Masses which had been offered for his repose afforded no benefit to him, because God, in punishment of his negligence, had applied them to other souls, who, while on earth, acted compassionately to their brethren in Purgatory.

XIX. Before concluding this instruction, let me, on bended knees, and with hands uplifted, implore all who read this little work not to close it till they have made a firm resolution of henceforth employing all possible diligence in assisting at Mass, and causing to be celebrated as many Masses as your means will permit, not only for the souls of the deceased, but also for your own. There are two motives which should determine you to adopt this counsel: the first, that you may obtain the blessing of a holy death, for it is the unalterable opinion of pious and learned men, that there is no more efficacious or desirable means for obtaining such a happiness than the holy Mass. It is related that Christ, our Lord, revealed to Saint Matilde, that whosoever, during life, has been accustomed to hear Mass devoutly, shall, in the hour of death, be comforted by the presence of Angels and his holy advocates, who will defend him triumphantly from all the assaults of the infernal fiends. Oh, what a happy and holy death must be yours, if, during life, you shall have endeavoured to hear Mass as often as possible!

The second motive that should animate you is, that you may get a speedy release from Purgatory and wing your way to eternal glory, since there can be no surer means of obtaining from God a grace so precious as that of going straight to Paradise without touching Purgatory, or at least of not being detained long there in purifying flames, than Indulgences and frequent celebrations of the holy Sacrifice. As for Indulgences, the Popes have drawn largely on the treasury of the Church by granting them copiously to all those who hear Mass with due devotion. Then as to the efficacy of the most holy sacrifice of the Mass in hastening the remission of the pains of Purgatory, what I have said heretofore is amply sufficient. But if you need anything more on this head let me remind you of the example and authority of that great servant of God, John d'Avila, the oracle of Spain, who, being interrogated in his last agony what he most longed for, and what he most earnestly wished to be done for him after his death, replied, " Masses, Masses!" And now, before dismissing this part of the subject, allow me to give you an advice which is of great moment. Cause all the Masses which you would wish to be offered for you after your death to be celebrated while you are still living in this world. Do not trust to those who survive you for the performance of this holy work. I am the more anxious to impress this on you, because St. Anselm affirms, that a single Mass heard or celebrated for your soul during life *may* be more beneficial to you than a thousand celebrated after your death. Let me quote the saint's words: *To hear even one Mass devoutly during one's life, or to give an alms for having it celebrated, is a far better thing than to bequeath alms for the celebration of a thousand after your decease.* A certain wealthy Genoese merchant, who, at his death, left nothing in suffrage for his soul, set proper value on this grand truth. Every one wondered that a man so rich, so pious, and so generous to all, could have been so cruel to himself at the hour of death, But after his interment there was found a little book, in his own handwriting, which showed how much he had done for his soul *during life.* Let me copy some of the entries: " Masses which I have caused to be celebrated for my soul, 2,000 *lire;* for dowries to poor girls, 10,000 ; for a certain pious institution, 200, &c., &c." At the end of this little memorandum he wrote as follows: " He who wishes to do good, let him do it while he is living; nor trust to those who may survive him." A very trite proverb tells us, that " a taper before gives more light than a torch behind." Let this edifying example be graven deeply on your heart, and ponder well the excellence and advantages of the holy Mass. Be amazed at the blindness in which you have lived hitherto, not setting due value on this treasure so great, so immense; a treasure, indeed, which has lain for you, alas! too long hidden. But now that you have learned its value, dismiss for ever from your mind, and still more from your lips, such scandalous propositions as "A Mass more or less counts for nothing." "'Tis a hardship to be obliged to assist at Mass on holidays." "The Mass of such a priest is as long as that of Holy Week: when he approaches the altar I get up and quit the church." Make a firm resolution to hear henceforth as many Masses as you can, and take heed that you hear them with due devotion. And in order that you may be enabled to do so, make use of the following practical and devout method which I have arranged for you. May God bless you.

CHAPTER II.

A SHORT AND DEVOUT METHOD OF HEARING MASS WITH GREAT FRUIT.

I. It was the opinion of St. John Chrysostom, as we have already stated in the foregoing instructions (and this opinion is approved and confirmed by St. Gregory, in the Fourth Book of Dialogues), that while the priest is celebrating holy Mass the skies open, and multitudinous legions of angels come down from Heaven to assist at the divine sacrifice. And St. Nilus, abbot and disciple of the said St. John Chrysostom, protested that he beheld, while the holy Doctor was celebrating, legions on legions of those celestial spirits assisting the sacred ministers during the performance of this most holy function. Now, let me point out to you the best method of assisting with great profit at holy Mass. Approach the church as if you were approaching Calvary, and prostrate yourself before the altar as you would before the throne of God in the society of his holy angels. See, therefore, how much modesty, reverence, and attention is required of us in order that we may gain the fruit and blessings which God is wont to grant to those who honour with devout deportment (internal and external) mysteries so sanctified.

II. We read that while the Jews were celebrating the sacrifices of the old law (which were, indeed, nothing but sacrifices of oxen, lambs, and other animals), it was edifying to witness with what earnestness, decorum, and silence, the entire body of the people assisted thereat; and although the multitude of the people was countless, independently of the seven hundred ministers who sacrificed, nevertheless, so still and solemn was the behaviour of all, that one would have imagined that the temple was empty, not as much as a whisper or a sigh being heard. Now, if those old shadowy sacrifices, which were nothing more than figures and types of the tremendous sacrifice of the new law, deserved so great respect and veneration, how great should be your silence, devotion, and attention, during the celebration of holy Mass, in which the very Immaculate Lamb, the Word made Flesh, is offered up for us. No one was more deeply impressed by this reflection than the great St. Ambrose, who (as Cesarius relates), when celebrating the divine mysteries, after reading the Gospel, used to turn to the people and exhort them, one and all, to devout recollectedness, commanding them at the same time to observe profoundest silence, not only by avoiding the merest whispering, but also by abstaining from *coughing* and every other sort of noise. And, indeed, the people paid attention to his instruction; and every one who assisted at the Mass he celebrated felt himself overawed by a holy dread, and was so intensely moved that he derived great fruit and increase of grace.

III. Such is the scope of this little work, whose only aim is to enlighten and excite every one who deigns to peruse it to embrace, with fervor of spirit, the practice and method of assisting at Mass which is here described. But, since the methods of assisting at Mass, which have been hitherto taught, are so various, each and all of them devout and most holy, as is evidenced by the numerous little books published for the greater benefit of the faithful, it is not my intention to do violence to your free will, but rather to leave you to select that one which is more agreeable to your devout inclination and capacity. I will merely act the part of your Guardian Angel, by suggesting to you the most profitable method, namely, that which, in my humble judgment, may prove to be the most useful and easiest. With this end in view, I will divide the whole matter into three classes.

IV. The first method of hearing holy Mass is that followed by those who, with their prayer book before them, accompany all the actions of the priest with the profoundest attention; reciting at each of them a vocal prayer, which they have in their book, and in this way they employ the whole time of holy Mass reading; and most assuredly, this is a most excellent method of assisting at Mass, nay, and a most profitable one, provided the reading be united with a profound consideration of the sacred mysteries. But as it involves an entire restraint, obliging the person assisting at the sacrifice to fix his mind on each of the holy ceremonies performed by the priest, and then to return with his eye to the book, in order to read the prayer corresponding to the mystery, it becomes in practice very wearying, and I think that few persevere in this method, or continue to adopt it for any considerable length of time, although in itself most useful. The weakness of our minds, which easily become overpowered by being obliged to reflect on each of the various actions performed by the priest at the altar, will account sufficiently for what I have said on this head. Nevertheless, let those who find it good for them, and derive spiritual profit by it, continue to observe it, particularly as God will not allow such a laborious application of the mind to be deprived of its fitting reward.

V. The second method of hearing holy Mass

SECOND METHOD OF HEARING MASS. 49

is that observed by those who, using no books, and abstaining from every sort of reading during the time of the holy sacrifice, fix their mental eye, enlightened by faith, on Jesus Crucified, and leaning against the tree of the cross, gather from it fruits of a sweet contemplation, spending the whole of that time in pious interior recollection, and sweetly meditating the sacred mysteries of our Lord's passion, which is not only represented, but is mystically carried out in that holy sacrifice. It is a fact beyond all doubt, that those who centre their mental faculties in God are enabled to perform heroic acts of Faith, Hope, Charity, and other virtues, and it is likewise certain that this method of hearing Mass is far more perfect than the first, nay, and more sweet and attractive. We have a happy illustration of this in the history of a good lay-brother, who used to say, that when hearing Mass he read only three letters. The first was black, that is to say, the consideration of his sins, which awakened in him confusion and repentance, and this occupied his meditations from the commencement of Mass to the Offertory. The second (letter) was red, that is to say, the meditation of the Passion of our Lord, contemplating that most precious blood which Jesus shed for us on Calvary, by suffering a death so full of agony, and in this he occupied his mind to the Communion. The third letter was white, because while the priest was communicating, he united himself mentally with Jesus in the sacrament, thus making a spiritual communion, after which he remained all absorbed in

God, meditating on the glory for which he hoped as fruit of that divine sacrifice. This simple-minded man heard Mass with great perfection, and I would to God that all might learn of him knowledge so sublime.

VI. The third method of hearing holy Mass with profit is to observe a middle course, that is to say, one which does not require the reading of many vocal prayers, as is laid down in the *first*, nor a very exalted spirit of contemplation, to which those aspire who follow the *second*. But if you consider it rightly, you will find that it is the one more in accordance with the spirit of the Church, which encourages us to unite our intentions to those of the celebrating priest, who is bound to offer the sacrifice for the four ends indicated in the preceding Instruction, this being, as St. Thomas (the Angelic) informs us, the most efficacious means of paying to God the four great debts which we owe to Him. Now, as you exercise, to a certain extent, the function of priest when you assist at Mass, you should be influenced, as much as possible, by the consideration of the four ends already indicated; and nothing will be more easy to you than this, if you only practise, during the time of holy Mass, the four offerings which shall be described to you hereafter. Here is the precise practical rule for you, if you are really anxious to realise it. Carry this little book about with you till you have learned the said offerings, or at least till you are well imbued with the *meaning* of the same, since it is not important that you should adhere strictly to the

THIRD METHOD OF HEARING MASS. 51

mere words; and as soon as Mass is begun, while the priest humbles himself at foot of the altar, saying the *Confiteor, &c.*, do you also (after a brief examination of conscience) excite in your heart an act of true contrition, asking of God pardon for your sins, and invoking the assistance of the Holy Ghost and of the Blessed Virgin, that you may be enabled to hear that Mass with entire reverence and devotion. Then divide it into four distinct periods of time, in order to pay during each of them the said four great debts, according to the following method and form.

VII. In the first period, which will be from the beginning to the Gospel, you will endeavour to pay the first debt, namely, of honoring and praising the majesty of God, which is worthy of infinite honor and infinite praise. Humble yourself, therefore, with Jesus, and sinking into the abyss of your own nothingness, acknowledge sincerely that you are a most miserable nothing before the majesty of God, and thus humbled interiorly, and also with a composed and modest exterior (for so should you always comport yourself at holy Mass), say:—"Ah, my God! I adore Thee for my Lord and the Master of my soul, I protest that all I am and have are Thy gifts. And, because Thy majesty merits infinite honor and homage, I, who am a poor, miserable creature, utterly incapable of paying the great debt which I owe to Thee, offer to Thee the humiliations and homage which Jesus presents to Thee on the altar; what Jesus does, I also intend to do. I humble and prostrate myself with Him before Thy majesty. I adore Thee with the same humiliations which Jesus offers to Thee. I am filled with joy and delight in reflecting that Jesus gives Thee, for me, infinite honor and homage." Then close the book, and continue exciting many internal acts of desire, that God should thus be infinitely honored; repeat them over and over again, frequently saying: "Yes, yes, my God, I am filled with joy for the infinite honor that redounds to thy Majesty from this most holy sacrifice. I am enraptured at it, and rejoice for it with all my powers, mental and physical." Nor need you adhere to the words, since it is better for you to use the language which your own devotion will dictate, while you are filled with recollection and united to your God. Oh! how fully will you pay your first debt by assisting at the first part of the Mass in this manner.

VIII. In the second period of time, which shall be from the Gospel to the Elevation, you will pay your second debt. Reflecting for a moment on the excessive enormity of your sins, and seeing the immense obligation which you have incurred by them to the divine Justice, say with heartfelt humility, " Behold, my God, the traitor who has so often rebelled against Thee. Ah! with a sorrowful heart, and with all the affections of my soul, I abhor and detest my most grievous sins, and I offer for them the same satisfaction which Jesus presents to Thee on the altar. I offer to Thee all the merits of Jesus, the blood of Jesus, Jesus entirely, God and man, who is here immolated again for me. And, since my Jesus Himself is, on this altar, my mediator and my advocate, and since, with His most precious blood, He implores pardon for me, I unite with the cry of His blood, and supplicate mercy for all my sins. The blood of Jesus cries for mercy, and my sorrowful heart also implores mercy. Ah! my dear God, if my tears do not move Thee, let at least the groans of my Jesus excite Thy pity. Why should He not obtain for me that mercy which He obtained for the whole human race upon the cross? Yes, I hope that for the sake of that most precious blood, Thou wilt pardon all my most grievous sins, which I will continue to bewail till my last breath." Having shut the book, repeat many of these acts of true, intimate, and profound contrition. Let your heart's affections have free course; and without noise of words but in your inmost heart, say to Jesus, "My dearest Jesus, give me the tears of Peter, the contrition of Magdalene, and the tender sorrow of the saints, who, although at one period sinners, were afterwards true penitents, in order that during this Mass I may obtain a general pardon for all my sins!" Entirely absorbed in God, make many acts of this sort, and rest assured, that you shall thus most fully discharge all the debts which you have contracted by so many grievous sins.

IX. In the third period of time, which shall be from the Elevation to the Communion, calling to mind the great and important blessings received from God, you will, in return for them, offer to Him a gift of infinite value, namely, the body and blood of Jesus Christ. Then you will invite all the angels and all the saints to thank God for you in the following or in some similar manner:—"Behold me, O my most loving God! loaded with the general and particular benefits which Thou hast bestowed, and wilt bestow upon me in time and eternity. I know that Thy mercies to me have been and are infinite. But I am ready to pay Thee for all, even to the last farthing. Behold the tribute of my gratitude, the payment which I offer for all Thy goodness, is this Divine blood, this most precious body, this innocent victim, which I present to Thee by the hands of the priest. I am certain that this oblation is sufficient to pay for all the gifts Thou hast conferred upon me; this gift of infinite value is an equivalent for all the favours I have ever received, now receive, or ever may receive from Thee. Ah! ye holy angels, and all ye blessed spirits, help me to thank my God; and, in thanksgiving for His great benefits, offer to Him not only this Mass, but also all the Masses that are now celebrated throughout the whole world, that His loving goodness may be fully recompensed for all the graces which He has bestowed, and is to bestow upon me now and for eternity. Amen." Oh, how pleasing to our good God will be such a heartfelt thanksgiving! Oh, how much will He be delighted with this sole oblation which, because it is of infinite value, has greater efficacy than all other offerings singly or collectively ! And in order to awaken deeper and livelier devotion in your heart, invite all the choirs of heaven to come to your assistance; nay, implore all those saints to whom you are most devout to intercede for you, and say from the depths of your heart, " Oh, all my holy patrons and intercessors, thank the goodness of God for me, so that I may not die with the sin of my ingratitude on my soul. Ah, beseech and supplicate Him to accept the weak throbbings of my heart, and to look benignly on the loving thanksgivings which my Jesus offers to Him for me in this Mass." Far from being satisfied with expressing yourself thus once only, repeat it over and over again, and rest convinced that by this means you will do much towards satisfying entirely this great debt. But in order to make success still more certain, you should, every morning, make the act of offering, which begins, "My eternal God" (I give it at the end of this little book), offering with this intention all the Masses that are being celebrated at the time throughout the entire world.

X. In the fourth period of time, which shall be from the Communion to the end of the Mass, after having communicated spiritually, while the priest is communicating sacramentally, in the manner which I will point out at the end of this chapter, contemplate God within your own heart, and then take courage to ask of Him many graces, being convinced that at that time Jesus unites Himself with you, nay, prays and supplicates for you. Therefore expand your heart, and ask not things of trifling value, but rather ask great graces; for, exceeding great, indeed, is the oblation of the Divine Son which you present to the Father. Address Him, then, with humbled heart in this manner, "My dear God, I acknowledge that I am utterly unworthy of thy favour; I confess my infinite unworthiness, and that, for my manifold and grievous sins, I do not deserve to be heard. But how canst Thou refuse to hear Thy Divine Son, who, on this altar, prays for me, and offers for me His blood and His life? Ah! my most loving God, hear the prayers of this my great Advocate, and, for his sake, grant me all the graces which Thou knowest to be necessary to secure the great affair of my eternal salvation. I am now encouraged to ask of Thee a general pardon of all my sins and the gift of final perseverance. Trusting in the prayers of my Jesus, I ask of Thee, O my God! all virtue, in an heroic degree, and all the efficacious helps necessary to make me truly a saint. I ask of Thee the conversion of all infidels and sinners, and particularly of those who are related to me. I ask of Thee the liberation, not of one soul only, but of all the souls in Purgatory; release them all, I beseech Thee, so that, through the efficacy of this divine sacrifice, that dungeon where they are being purified may be emptied. Convert the souls of all those who sojourn in this miserable world, till it becomes for Thee a paradise of delights; and grant that, after having loved, reverenced, and praised Thee here below, we may finally come to praise and bless Thee for all eternity. Amen." Ask, also with fervor, blessings for yourselves, for your children, and for your friends, kinsmen, and acquaintances; ask relief for all your necessities, spiritual as well as temporal; ask for the fulness of all good, and release from all evils, for our holy Church; and do not ask with tepidity, but with great confidence, and rest assured that your prayers, united with those of Jesus, will most certainly be heard. When Mass is terminated make an act of thanksgiving, as in the *agimus tibi gratias*, to God, and leave the church with heart contrite as if you were descending the hill of Calvary. Now answer me this question: If all the Masses at which you have assisted hitherto had been heard by you in this manner, would not your souls have been enriched with treasures beyond counting? Oh, what a loss you have sustained while you assisted at the unbloody sacrifice, looking curiously about you, watching who came in and went out of the church; nay, sometimes whispering to one another, half asleep, or, at most, muttering over a few vocal prayers without the least interior recollection! Resolve, therefore, to adopt this most sweet and easy method of hearing Mass with fruit, which consists in discharging the four great debts which you have contracted with God; and rest thoroughly convinced, that in a very little time you will earn for yourself a rich accumulation of the choicest graces. Adopt this method and it will never again be your misfortune to say, "A Mass more or less counts for nothing."

XI. As regards the way of making a spiritual

communion while the priest is communicating in the Mass, it is necessary that you should be informed of what the holy Council of Trent teaches on this subject; namely, that we can receive the most holy Sacrament in three ways: the first, only sacramentally; the second, only spiritually; the third, both sacramentally and spiritually. Here I will not speak of the first (way), that is to say, of the communion of those who, like Judas, receive the body of the Lord unworthily; nor of the third, which is common to all those who communicate worthily, or in the state of grace; but I will speak of the second, which is peculiar to those who, as the holy Council says, not being able to receive the body of the Lord sacramentally, receive it spiritually, with acts of a lively faith and a fervent charity, and with a burning desire to unite themselves to that supreme good, thus rendering themselves capable of receiving the fruit of this divine Sacrament. In order, therefore, to facilitate such a holy practice, I pray you to ponder well on what I am going to say. At the moment when the priest is about to communicate in holy Mass, do you (observing at the same time, a perfect composure, external, as well as internal), excite in your heart an act of sincere contrition, and humbly striking your breast in acknowledgment of your unworthiness to receive so great a grace, make all those acts of love, self-offering, and humility, with all the rest that you are accustomed to make when you communicate sacramentally, and then yearn, with an earnest longing, to receive your adorable Jesus who has deigned to veil Himself in the Sacrament for your spiritual and temporal welfare. And in order to make your faith still more lively, imagine that the Mother of God, or some one of your patron saints administers the adorable particle to you; think that you are actually receiving it, and after embracing Jesus in your heart, say to him over and over again with heart-felt words dictated by love, "Come, dearest Jesus, come into this, my poor unhappy heart, come and satiate my longings: come and sanctify my soul: come, my sweetest Jesus, come!" And having said this, or something like it, remain silent, contemplating your good God within you, and—just as if you had received *sacramentally*—adore Him, and thank Him; nay, and make all those acts which you are accustomed to make after the sacramental communion.

Now you are to bear in mind, that this blessed and holy spiritual communion (alas, so little practised by Christians in our times!) is a treasure which enriches the soul with inestimable wealth; and, as very many spiritual writers inform us,[*] it is so useful that it is capable of producing the very same graces which sacramental communion produces, and, in some instances, greater. For although, in fact, sacramental communion (that is to say, when you receive the adorable particle *really*), is, of its own nature, capable of producing greater fruit, because being the Sacrament, it

---

[*] Among others, Father Rodriguez, Christian Perfection, p. 2, Tract 8, c. 15.

possesses virtue *ex opere operato;** nevertheless, a soul can make a spiritual communion with so much humility, love, and devotion, as to deserve greater grace than another soul which communicates *sacramentally*, but without dispositions so entirely excellent.

Our divine Redeemer has so manifested his delight at this practice of spiritual communion, that on several occasions, and with signal miracles, He has deigned to give willing ear to the pious longings of his chosen servants; sometimes administering the holy communion to them with His own hands, as was the case with blessed Clare of Montefalco, Saint Catherine of Siena, and Saint Liduina; sometimes by the hands of angels, as to my patron, St. Bonaventure, called the Seraphic Doctor, and to the two holy bishops, Onoratus and Firminus; and sometimes also through the medium of the blessed Mother of God, who wished to administer the holy communion with her own hands to the blessed Silvester. Nor should we wonder at these prodigies of love, because spiritual communion inflames the soul with love of God, nay, unites it to God, and disposes it to receive His most signal favours. How, then, with this truth so plainly before you, can you continue to be so cold and insensible? and what excuse can you allege to exempt yourself from such a devout practice? Ah! make your choice at once, and, furthermore, bear in mind that this holy spiritual communion gives you this advantage over the sacramental communion,

---

* i.e., by its own intrinsic efficacy.

that the latter can be made only once each day, while the spiritual communion may be repeated at all the Masses at which you assist. Besides, it may be made even when you are not at Mass, at morning, mid-day, evening, or night; in the church, in your own house, without asking permission of your confessor. In a word, so often as you reduce to practice what I have here laid down for your instruction, so often will you make a spiritual communion, and by this holy custom you will enrich yourself with graces, and merits, and every good.

Here, then, I have now unfolded to you the object of this unpretending little book. Its simple aim is to kindle in the hearts of all those who peruse it a holy desire, that there may be introduced into the Catholic world, the devout custom of hearing holy Mass every day with the most solid piety and devotion, and that at each time you assist at the holy sacrifice each and all of you may make a spiritual communion. Oh, what blessings would come upon you if this end were attained! Then, indeed, I should hope to behold throughout the whole universe, all that holy fervour which was witnessed in that golden age of the primitive Church, when the faithful assisted every day at the holy sacrifice, and every day communicated sacramentally. If you are not worthy of such a holy privilege, at least assist at Mass every day, and every day make a spiritual communion. If I succeed in winning you who peruse these pages, I will imagine that I have gained the entire world, and I will regard my humble labour as well expended. But in order to remove once and for ever all the excuses which some persons are wont to make for not hearing holy Mass, the following chapter will display to your view various examples applicable to persons of every condition, to prove that if they deprive themselves of so great a good it is through their own fault, their tepidity and want of zeal in serving God; and that the remorse which such shortcomings must cause them at the hour of death shall indeed be great.

CHAPTER III.

VARIOUS EXAMPLES TO INDUCE ALL THE FAITHFUL, OF EVERY STATE AND CONDITION, TO HEAR HOLY MASS DAILY.

NUMBERLESS are the excuses which those who attend holy Mass *reluctantly* allege for their tepidity. You will find them wholly devoted to their avocations, all-absorbed in worldly pursuits, and intent on promoting the most sordid interests. For these every sort of fatigue is trifling; nor is there any amount of labour which they are not willing to endure, while for assisting at the holy sacrifice, which is the greatest affair of all, you will find them heedless and cold, with a hundred frivolous pretexts at hand, such as, serious occupations, weak health, family broils, want of time, multiplicity of engagements, &c. In a word, if holy Church did not compel them, under pain of mortal sin, to hear Mass at least on festivals, God knows whether they would ever enter a church or bend a knee before an altar! Oh, shame! Oh, bitter disgrace to our times! Wretched we! How have we declined from the fervour of the early Christians, who, as has been related above, assisted at the holy sacrifice every day, and refreshed themselves with the bread of angels by communicating sacramentally. And yet, they were not exempt from business and toil; nay, by this very means, they were enabled to attend to their worldly concerns properly, thus promoting their every interest, spiritual and temporal. Blind world, when wilt thou open thine eyes to an error so palpable! Christian soul, arouse thee —shake off tepidity! and let this be thy most cherished, thy most constant devotion—to hear holy Mass every day, and to make a spiritual communion at its celebration. In order to secure a consummation so holy, I know no means more efficacious than example; for it is an indubitable maxim that we are influenced by example; and everything comes easy to us when we see it practised by our equals and acquaintances. "What," said St. Augustine, rebuking his own waywardness, "are you not able to do what has been done by those men and those women?"* I will, therefore, lay before you various examples relating to distinct classes of persons, and by this means I trust to be able to gain you all.

* Conf. l. 8, c. xi.

§. 1.

EXAMPLES TO INDUCE PRIESTS TO OFFER THE HOLY SACRIFICE OF THE MASS EVERY MORNING, EXCEPT IN CASE OF SOME LEGITIMATE IMPEDIMENT.

AWAKEN, oh! ye priests of Christ, and take heed, in the first place, that the eye of your intention be pure and entirely fixed on God. For this purpose I adjure you, before you commence Mass, to renew, at least mentally, the four ends already pointed out and prescribed by the Angelic Doctor, and in the "*Memento*," after applying the holy sacrifice for those to whom you are under obligation, make succinctly those offerings to the Most High, directing them to those holy ends for which the Mass has been instituted—that is, to honour God, to thank Him, to make satisfaction to Him, and to obtain from His goodness all the blessings which we need; observe all possible diligence in celebrating the adorable Sacrifice with profoundest modesty, recollectedness, and attention, reverently, without haste, taking ample time to pronounce all the words correctly and distinctly, and performing all the sacred ceremonies with that gravity and decorum which is required of you. Now I tell you, that if the words are not pronounced distinctly, and if the holy ceremonies are not performed with gravity and strict observance of the Rubric, instead of being an aid to piety and religion your neglect or indifference will scandalise those who assist at the sacred function. It should be the celebrant's chiefest care to observe the most unbroken interior recollectedness, attending to the sense of the words which he pronounces, relishing their signification and spirit, and making in his inmost heart acts of various virtues, corresponding to their holy inspirations. Thus will the priest be enabled to pour, as it were, additional devotion into the hearts of those who assist at the holy Sacrifice, and thus will he be enabled to derive great profit from it for himself. Having premised all this, and taking it for granted that every priest acknowledges the excellence of this method of celebrating, I would exhort them, one and all, to make a firm and inflexible resolution of offering the divine sacrifice every morning; for if the laity were accustomed to communicate *daily* in the time of the primitive Church, with how much more reason are we to believe that the priest should celebrate daily? "Daily do I immolate the Immaculate Lamb to God," said St. Andrew to the tyrant, and St. Cyprian, in one of his Epistles, writes, "We, priests, who *daily* immolate the sacrifice to God." St. Gregory the Great, writing of St. Cassius, Bishop of Narni, informs us, that God commanded one of the holy prelate's chaplains to tell him, that he did well by celebrating the holy sacrifice daily; that his devotion was grateful in His sight, and that He would reward it amply in heaven. Now, on the other hand, what are we to say of those priests who, through merest negligence, omit the daily oblation of the holy Mass? Who could ever describe adequately the great loss which they inflict on the Church? Let the maxim of the Venerable

F

Bede be graven on your heart, " The priest who, without a legitimate impediment, fails to celebrate daily, deprives, as far as it is in his power to do so, the holy Trinity of praise and glory, the angels of joy, sinners of pardon, the just of aid and grace, the souls in Purgatory of suffrage and alleviation, the Church of immense benefit, and himself of medicine and cure." Where will you find me a robber so unequalled, who, at one swoop, commits such extensive plunder, as does the priest, who, without a legitimate impediment, neglects to celebrate, and thus despoils the living and the dead, nay, the whole Church, of so many blessings? Nor, will it avail him to urge, that he is overwhelmed by occupations. The blessed Ferdinand, Archbishop of Granada, and who was also the prime minister of that kingdom, and consequently engrossed with multitudinous occupations, was wont, nevertheless, to celebrate every morning. The Cardinal of Toledo intimated to him, that the Court regretted that he celebrated each day, overwhelmed as he was with so many serious occupations;* but the servant of God replied, " 'Tis precisely for that reason that I offer the holy sacrifice every morning; for their Highnesses have imposed so heavy a burden on my shoulders, that I can find no better support against being weighed down to the ground than the holy sacrifice of the altar, from which I derive strength to bear the onerous responsibility placed upon me." And of far less avail is a certain species of humility, as we find exemplified in the case of

* Rodriguez, p. 2, Tract 7, c. 16.

St. Peter Celestine, who, on account of the exalted estimate which he had formed of so great a mystery, wished to abstain from celebrating daily. While meditating this half-formed resolution, a holy abbot, from whom he had received the habit of a monk, appeared to him, and spoke thus, in a tone of imperious remonstrance: "Where in all heaven will you find me a seraph who is worthy to celebrate? God has made men and not angels ministers of the holy sacrifice, and men are subject to a thousand imperfections. Humble yourself as much as you will, for it is good, but celebrate daily, for such is the wish of the Most High." But in order that the frequent celebration may not tend to diminish the due reverence, you should labour to imitate those saints whose modesty and attention shone out more lustrously during the august function. The great and far-famed Archbishop, St. Herbert, was overpowered by such extraordinary devotion whilst celebrating Mass, that he looked like an angel of Paradise. St. Laurence Giustiniani, while saying Mass, seemed to have grown, as it were, immoveable at the altar; his eyes flowed with tears, and his entire soul was centered in God. But St. Francis de Sales may be regarded as the most sublime example of all; for never was there an ecclesiastic who, at the altar, comported himself with greater majesty, reverence, or recollectedness than that which he exhibited. No sooner was he clothed in the sacerdotal vestments than he divested himself of every thought that had not direct relation to the divine function he was going to perform, and once that his foot touched the first step of the altar, his whole interior and exterior put on an angelic expression that captivated the hearts of all who beheld him.

But how came it that those saints were able to find so much comfort and refreshment in the celebration of holy Mass? Simply because they celebrated with proper dispositions, just as if they had been in presence of the entire court of heaven. Let me illustrate this by telling you what on one occasion happened to St. Bonitus, Bishop of Clermont. The holy prelate was one night praying in his church, when the blessed Mother of God, attended by choirs of celestial spirits, appeared within the sacred precincts. Some of the angels attending on our Lady asked her, " Who is to celebrate the holy sacrifice at daybreak?" and she answered, " Bonitus, my well-loved servant." The holy bishop hearing his name spoken retired, filled with dread, and wishing to hide himself leant against a stone, which, on the instant, became soft as clay, by a special miracle, and took the impression of the saint's body, which it has retained ever since. But his humility only served to make him the more worthy, for he was constrained to celebrate in presence of the great Mother of God, and was attended, during the celebration, by all the foresaid heavenly spirits. After Mass the Blessed Virgin bestowed on him an Alb, of purest white, and of texture so fine, that there never was anything that could be compared to it, and which, even to this day, is preserved as a most precious relic. Now, only fancy with what modesty, recollection, and love he must have celebrated that Mass. But should this example appear too sublime for your imitation, contemplate that given you by the glorious St. Vincent Ferrer, who was accustomed to offer the holy sacrifice every morning before preaching, and who always brought with him to the altar two grand perfections, unblemished interior purity and an external cleanliness, of the most edifying character. In order to secure the former, he made it a rule to approach the tribunal of Penance every morning; and I would counsel you, O priests who desire to taste of God in celebrating the august mysteries, to imitate him in this respect. Some of you spend half hours reading devout little books, in order to prepare yourselves for the holy sacrifice, while, by making a brief examination of conscience, and exciting yourselves to a heartfelt contrition for some sin of your past life (other matter not presenting itself), you could thus acquire that purity of conscience so desirable. Here, then, is the most fitting preparation that you can make for the saying of Mass, confess your sins every morning. Away with all scruples, and take heed to this, my counsel. Oh, what a superabundance of merits will not this enable you to acquire; and how cordially will you thank me hereafter in a glorious eternity! In order to provide for the latter (external cleanliness), St. Vincent Ferrer invariably caused the altar to be adorned with all possible pomp and decorum; and as he always celebrated the holy mysteries in presence of vast congregations, he took great care that everything, vestments and sacred utensils, pertaining to the altar should be kept scrupulously clean.

Now, let me tell you that I can hardly refrain from weeping, when I call to mind what I have witnessed when giving missions, not only in the churches of rural districts, but also in those of the great towns. Alas! to what am I to attribute such shocking neglect? Must I attribute it to the avarice, negligence, or irreligion of the ministers? I know not; but this I know, that I have seen Vestments, Corporals, Purificatories, and other requirements of the altar, so filthy and stained, that they almost turned the stomachs of priests as well as laymen, who could not look on them without feelings of horror. "Nothing," says the holy Council of Lateran, "can be so absurd as to be heedless of that want of neatness in *sacred things*, which you would not tolerate in *profane things*." For my part I cannot bear such criminal neglect; and I now warn ye, Sacristans, Parish Priests, and Rectors, that I will, one day, make you accountable before God's tribunal for your horrible negligence. How will you say that you have not been guilty of a mortal sin, if you furnish the altar with linens which you would not place on a profane table? And now, ye Bishops, Prelates, and Visitors, what are ye doing? Why, when you find, on your visitations, foul Purificatories, Corporals half consumed by mice, and chalice-veils begrimed, why,

I ask, don't you tear them to pieces under the very eyes of such negligent Parish Priests? Why don't you punish them to the utmost extent of your power? You will tell me, perhaps, that you find everything neat and in good order in the churches. Take heed that you are not deceived by such representations; and let me advise you to adopt the very clever stratagem of a most zealous bishop, who, when on his visitation, entered a Sacristy, which was amply furnished with all requirements, Chasubles of cloth of gold, Albs of the finest texture, and all other things in perfect keeping. Now, said he to the Parish Priest, I command you, under pain of suspension from all priestly faculties, to be incurred on the very instant, not to allow a single one of all these things to be removed from your church under any pretext! Will you believe it?—the Parish Priest had borrowed all those things for the occasion!

I am well aware that the poverty of many churches is ample excuse for the absence of rich altar apparel, adorned with gold and silver; but how can poverty be an excuse for the absence of neatness and cleanliness? My seraphic patron, St. Francis, cherished such glowing zeal for the holy sacrifice that, although loving holy poverty beyond all things, he insisted, nevertheless, that the sacristies and the altars should be kept in the most scrupulous cleanliness, and still more so, the sacred furniture that was used about the adorable Sacrament. Indeed, with his own hands he very often swept the floor of his church. St. Charles Borromeo, too, in his exhortations, showed himself so exact in those particulars (descending frequently to what might seem merest minutiæ), that he astonishes all those who read his life. In fact, the ever blessed Mother of God herself in person was pleased to express her wishes regarding this matter when revealing herself to St. Brigid. She said to her, "Mass should not be celebrated except with cleanest vestments, which inspire devotion by their propriety and neatness."

Before terminating this paragraph, I feel myself called on to say a few words regarding the minister who serves Mass. In our days this office has devolved on mere boys and pious youths, although the grandest monarchs of the world are not worthy of such an honor. St. Bonaventure tells us that this is an angelic office, because, during the divine oblation, many angels are actually present who serve God in that august function. The glorious saint Matilde had a vision of the soul of a lay brother crowned with ineffable glory, because he had always behaved with extraordinary diligence and devotion while serving every Mass at which he was able to be present. And St. Thomas of Aquin—that light of the schools—justly appreciating the hidden treasure enfolded in this office of serving at the divine sacrifice, would not be content after offering it if he was not allowed to serve the Mass of another priest. And Thomas More, the Chancellor of England, took the greatest delight in this holy work of serving at Mass; so much so, that on one occasion, when taunted by some minister of state, who said that King Henry would be offended if he learned that the Chancellor had so humbled himself, the latter replied, " My lord the king cannot be offended with me for the service I render to *his* Lord; nay, to the King of kings and Lord of lords." Certain persons, and some of them belonging to religious communities, are very much abashed at the idea of having to perform this holy office; so much so, indeed, that it is often necessary to almost compel them to serve Mass. But instead of being ashamed to serve at the altar, should they not rather rival each other in anxiety to carry the Missal, and have the honor of performing a service so devout in its nature that the angels and blessed in heaven themselves envy them? Great diligence, however, should be employed in instructing the persons who are permitted to serve Mass. Let them be taught to keep their eyes bent downwards, and to observe that strict decorum which is inspired by a profound sense of the majesty of the august sacrifice. Let their whole exterior exhibit deepest reverence and compunction. Let them be taught to pronounce the words *distinctly*, slowly, and in a tone not too low to be heard by the priest, nor so loud as to distract those who are celebrating at the other altars. Special care should be taken to exclude certain thoughtless little boys who are given to levity, and who, instead of performing the office of servitor devoutly, often indulge in trivialities and noise, so as to distract the celebrant. My earnest prayer to God is, that He will deign to enlighten men of good dispositions to give edification by undertaking an office so laudable and so holy. Surely the noblest and the wisest are they who should set the example to others.

§. 2.

EXAMPLES OF VARIOUS PRINCES, KINGS, AND EMPERORS.

The examples of those who hold distinguished positions in the world, generally speaking, have more influence than the piety of private individuals, how great soever it may be; for, indeed, nothing can be more true than the aphorism which says, " that every one imitates the example of the court." And oh, what a long series of those examples left us by the great ones of this world might I adduce to animate all those who read these pages to walk in their footsteps by assisting daily at the holy sacrifice of the Mass! Let us content ourselves, however, by glancing at a few of them. Constantine the Great not only heard Mass daily in his palace, but even in his military expeditions, amid the clang of arms and the camp he was always provided with a portable altar, in order that the holy sacrifice might be celebrated continually. To this, doubtless, he was indebted for his most splendid victories. The Emperor Lothaire observed the same holy practice; for he made it a rule in time of war, as well as of peace, to hear three Masses every day. And the pious King

Henry the Third of England also daily heard three Masses, at which his entire court assisted with the most exemplary devotion. And God rewarded him most signally even in this life; for he swayed the sceptre fifty-six years. Now it is not necessary to dwell on the history of the past in order to show how great was the piety of the English kings, or their assiduity in assisting at the holy sacrifice, since we have only to call to mind the profound devotion of Maria Clementina, that most pious queen whose demise Rome has not yet ceased to lament, and who, as she herself often confided to me, esteemed no happiness equal to that of assisting at Mass. In fact, she was accustomed to hear many Masses every day, and while engaged at this holy work she remained immoveable, dispensing with cushions and kneeling-stools, so that she seemed a veritable statue of piety. This practice, so devout and so admirable, kindled in her heart such glowing love for Jesus in the Sacrament, that she usually attended every day at three or four benedictions of the Most Holy, driving at full speed through the streets of Rome, in her carriage, in order to be in time at the different churches. And oh, how many tears did this great and devout lady shed in her holy hunger for this Bread of Angels! A hunger, indeed, so vehement as to cause her to languish day and night, because she felt her heart constantly turning towards that object on which her love was centred. Nevertheless, God so willed it that her anxious desires in this particular should not be gratified; and this he ordained in order to render her love heroic, nay, to make her a martyr of divine love, for I believe that this unsatisfied desire of receiving holy communion accelerated her death, as may be manifestly concluded from the last letter which she wrote to me when her dissolution was nigh. But one thing is certain, namely—that, although deprived of frequent communion, she was not deprived of its merit, since she found in spiritual communion that ecstatic love which she could not indulge in sacramental communion. Not only during the celebration of Mass, but frequently throughout the day, she repeated her spiritual communion with exceeding great joy of soul, rigidly adhering to the form which I have laid down in the preceding chapter.

Now, answer me, will not this example (which we have witnessed with our own eyes, and which, in our own times, has been admired by every one in Rome) be sufficient to smother in their throats the idle excuses of all those who make so much difficulty about hearing Mass daily, and making a spiritual communion during its celebration. Although it is not in my power to persuade you to imitate this pious queen, by devoting all the affections of your heart to intense desires of receiving Jesus in the Sacrament, yet, I would exhort you to imitate her in employing the labour of your hands, as she was often wont to do, to provide sacred furniture for poor churches. This example, indeed, has been followed in Rome by numerous ladies of every rank, who deem it a delightful recreation to elaborate, with their own hands, ornaments and furniture for the altars.

Nor is Rome the only city in which such pious works are performed, for I could name a great Princess (living elsewhere), of highest rank and most noble birth, and not less illustrious for her piety, who, every morning, assists at many Masses, and very frequently occupies all the ladies of her household in working for the altars, so as to be able to send whole chests of Corporals, Purificatories, and such like necessaries, to missionaries and preachers, in order that they may be distributed among poor churches, and that thus the holy sacrifice may everywhere be celebrated with fitting splendour, cleanliness, and decorum. What should now prevent me from exclaiming, ye great ones of this world, here you behold a sure means of winning the kingdom of heaven. And yet, tell me, I beseech you, how do you act? Why do you not open your hands, and prove your liberality by bestowing abundant alms on so many churches that are steeped in poverty? It will not do to tell me that the treasury is half empty, that the taxes are insufficient, or that the revenue is every day decreasing. I will point out to you a very ready method of providing for God's altars, without prejudice to the dignity of your estate. Here it is ready to your hand. A horse the fewer in your stables, a footman the fewer on your carriage box, a butler the fewer in your summer residence, and thus you will have effected a considerable saving, which will enable you to relieve the necessities of so many poor parishes. You summon diets and congresses, you enter into treaties, and convoke councils of war, to secure the welfare of your provinces, and yet all this does not prosper, whereas one single thought, suggesting a middle course, might adjust a negotiation, and that negotiation carried out might save a whole kingdom. But that thought, so replete with advantages, whence is it to come? From God—ponder well what I tell you—it must come from God alone. And what is the most efficacious means for obtaining it? The holy Mass. Therefore, hear as many Masses as you can, cause many Masses to be celebrated for your pious intentions, furnish the altars with sacred vessels and suitable vestments, and by doing this you will find a most marvellous providence of God keeping guard over you, a providence, indeed, that will protect your States, and render you happy in time and in eternity.

Let us conclude the paragraph by quoting the example of St. Wenceslaus, King of Bohemia, which all of you should imitate in part, if not to its full extent. This holy King was not satisfied with assisting daily at numerous Masses, kneeling on an uncarpeted floor, nor with serving, in person, the celebrant priests, an office in which he comported himself with humility far greater than might be found in any cleric who has only been admitted to *tonsure*, the least of minor orders; but along with this, he contributed to the sacred altars the richest jewels of his treasury, and the most costly stuffs from the royal wardrobe. With his own royal hands he was wont to make the Hosts which were to be used in the holy sacrifice; and with this object before his eyes, regardless of his royal dignity, he, himself, employed those hands, destined to wield sceptres, in cultivating a field, guiding a plough, sowing the seed, and gathering the crop. He then ground the wheat carefully, prepared the flour for baking, nay, and formed the hosts which were to be consecrated, and which he presented to the priests with the most humble reverence, in order that they might be converted into the divine body of our Saviour. Oh, hands worthy, indeed, to wield the sceptre of the entire world! But how was he rewarded for a devotion so tender? Almighty God caused the Emperor, Otho I., to cherish such unequalled love for this holy King, that he authorized him to quarter in his arms the imperial device, a black eagle in an argent field, a favor which he would not grant to any other potentate. Thus did God, through means of the Emperor Otho, reward the great devotion which Wenceslaus entertained for the most holy sacrifice. But far more splendidly was he recompensed by the King of Heaven, when, by a most glorious martyrdom, he obtained a diadem of everlasting glory. Thus, in return for his love and veneration of holy Mass, was he doubly crowned in this life, and in the kingdom of heaven. Reflect and resolve.

§. 3.

EXAMPLES FOR LADIES IN HIGH STATION.

A LADY who enters church pompously, and bedizened with a variety of ornaments, is likely to attract the attention of those who are there assembled, and, in some instances (may heaven avert such impiety!) even hearts, thus robbing God of the profound and undivided homage that is due to Him. Hence it would be superfluous to cite examples in order to induce such ladies to hear Mass every day; for, in fact, they are only too anxious to be seen in the churches. My grandest object is to teach them with what great modesty and reverence they should comport themselves in the house of God, particularly during the celebration of the holy sacrifice; and, indeed, it affords me great pleasure to say, that I have been greatly edified by the demeanour of many ladies of distinguished rank, who enter the churches and kneel before God's altars, attired modestly, as becometh the holiness of the place. But, on the other hand, I must confess that I have been greatly scandalized by some vain, thoughtless creatures, who, with plumed head-gear, gaudy habiliments, and deportment such as is usual on the stage of a theatre, would almost make one think that they were goddesses of a heathen temple! In order, therefore, to awaken in this latter class of persons that reverential awe which should influence them during the celebration of the august mysteries, I will here relate a miraculous vision which is described in the life of the blessed Ivetta, a Flemish noblewoman. Assisting at Mass one day, she found herself kneeling beside a young lady who was dressed in the height of the prevailing fashion. Now God was pleased so to enlighten his blessed servant Ivetta, that she actually beheld the workings of that young woman's heart, and had the clearest perception of all the thoughts—some of which were of the most abominable sort—that entered and passed through her mind, without any restraint. Hovering about this vain young woman were countless fiends, who seemed to attend her as her hired servants; some of them arranging the drapery of her robe, others taking special care of her glittering trinkets, as though this was their whole duty. At length the fashionable lady presented herself at the communion rail to receive the holy sacrament. The priest descended the altar steps with the ciborium in his hands, and Blessed Ivetta beheld, as it were in a vision, the reluctance with which Christ suffered Himself to be sacramentally administered to the sinner.

But you will say to me, "I do not belong to a class so contemptible and so depraved," and, indeed, I believe you are stating what is the truth; but yet, that style of dress, so unsuited to the solemn majesty of God's temple—those trinkets and perfumes—that all-absorbing wish to be seen and to be admired—to have people say of you, "how surpassingly beautiful! how splendidly dressed! how graceful in her movements!" Where shall I find words strong enough to denounce such scandals? I tell you that vanities of this kind are an abomination in the sight of God. I tell you that by such conduct you turn His house into a den of robbers. So you must be aware that you rob Christ of honour, by distracting not only the virtuously-disposed members of the congregation, but even the very priests ministering at the altar! Ah, then, enter into yourselves, and resolve to imitate Saint Elizabeth, Queen of Hungary, who would go in all regal state to Mass, but on reaching the sacred threshold, would remove the diadem from her head, the rings from her fingers, and thus divested of all royal ornament, would kneel, covered with a veil, so modest in her demeanour that she was never known to glance around her or turn away her eyes for a single moment from the altar. And so pleasing to Almighty God was her devout conduct, that He deigned to make His approval of it manifest to the entire congregation; for, on one occasion, during the celebration of the holy sacrifice she was enveloped in a luminous glory that dazzled the eyes of all those who were present, and made every one regard her as an angel of paradise. Yes, imitate this noble example, and be assured that you will thus render yourselves pleasing in the sight of God and men, and the fruits which you shall gain from the holy sacrifice will be ineffable blessings in time and in eternity.

§. 4.

FOR WOMEN IN GENERAL.

GREAT, certainly, is the fruit to be gained by assisting at the holy sacrifice, as we have shown in the preceding Instruction; but there are certain circumstances frequently occurring which render it inexpedient for some women to go to Mass on ordinary days. You who are nursing an infant, or are bound by an obligation of justice or of charity to attend a person lying sick, or you who have an irreligious or ill-tempered husband who forbids you to leave the house, you should not be disquieted about it, or what is worse, disobey. For, although holy Mass is indeed a thing than which nothing can be holier, and as we have demonstrated, productive of countless blessings, nevertheless, obedience, and the denial of your own will, are better in the circumstances to which we have alluded. Furthermore, for your consolation be it told you, that by *obeying* you redouble your gain and merit; since the goodness of God, in such a case, will not only reward your obedience, but will give you credit for the Mass just as if you had actually heard it, because He is fully satisfied with your holy intention. On the other hand, disobedience must deprive you of one and the other merit, for it would prove that you found more pleasure in acting according to the promptings of your own will, than that of God, who has expressly declared in the Holy Scriptures that "obedience is better than victims," or, in other words, that he is more satisfied with obedience than with Masses and sacrifices which are not of precept.

But what if you should go to Mass to indulge in idle conversations, curiosity, and voluntary distractions, and thus return to your home empty-handed and unbenefited by the august sacrifice? So did it befall a certain peasant-woman who lived in a cottage hard by the village-church. She, in order to obtain from God the concession of a favour on which she had set her heart, vowed and resolved to hear a great number of Masses in the course of the year. Therefore, whenever she heard the bell inviting the people to the divine sacrifice, she would instantly lay aside whatever work she had in hands, and hurry off to the church through sleet or snow, utterly regardless of the inclemency of the season. On her return home, in order to keep a punctual and accurate account of the Masses (so that she might not fail of a single one of the number to which she bound herself), she invariably deposited a bean in a little box which she kept in a secret place. At the close of the year, fully assured that she had complied with her vow, presented a great offering of homage to God, and acquired no trifling merit for herself, she proceeded to open the little box, when lo! of all the beans that she deposited there, she found only a single one. Overwhelmed with astonishment, she was sadly grieved, so much so indeed, that she addressed herself to God, while tears streamed from her eyes, saying, "O Lord! how happens it, that of all the Masses I have heard, I only find the mark of one? Surely, I never failed to be present at the altar, even when it was most inconvenient for me to leave my cottage! Surely, I never allowed bad weather, rain, frost, or any other obstacle to keep me from going to church!" God, indeed, inspired her to go and consult a wise and pious priest, who asked her how she had conducted herself when going to church, and with what devotion, interior and exterior, she had assisted at the holy sacrifice? To these questions she replied thus: "On my way to the church I used to gossip with my acquaintances about our domestic concerns, and other things of less serious importance, and when kneeling at the altar I confess that I was in the habit of whispering to this one and that, having my thoughts always fixed on my little household or farm." "Here, then," replied the priest, "you state the exact cause of the loss of so many Masses; gossiping, curiosity, and voluntary distractions have robbed you of so much merit; either the demon has carried off the records you deposited in the box, for his own purposes, or your guardian angel has removed them in order that you might discover how good works may turn out utterly worthless, if not performed with the proper spirit. Give God thanks, nevertheless, that you have heard one Mass as you should, and that that one has been profitable to you." Now here make a serious reflection, and say to yourself, "Who knows how many of all the Masses I have heard during my life may have been acceptable and agreeable to God?" What does your conscience answer? If it tells you that very, very few of them may have been beneficial to you in God's sight, lose no time in employing the only true remedy, and resolve, forthwith, to amend your conduct for the future. But if, unhappily (which God forbid!), you may have been one of those wretched creatures who do the work of the devil, by recruiting souls for him even in God's consecrated temple, listen to the following appalling fact, and tremble. 'Tis related in a book, entitled, '*Dormi Sicuro*,' that a certain woman, reduced to abject poverty, wandered about in a state of despair through unfrequented places, where a devil appeared to her and spoke thus—" You were once well off in the world, and I feel for your altered circumstances; do now what I bid you, and you may rest assured that I will make you as comfortable as you were formerly. Whenever you go to church entertain the persons who kneel beside you with idle, impertinent gossip; do all you can to distract them by whispering, and such like irreverences, and you may be sure that I will keep my promise." The wretched woman consented to the proposal, and gave herself, body and soul, to do the devil's work, in which she succeeded wonderfully; for she maintained such incessant chattering with whatever person happened to kneel beside her, and employed so many artful stratagems to distract every one within her reach, that it was wholly impossible to attend piously to the divine sacrifice, or listen with due reverence to the priest preaching the word of God. But it was not long till the avenging hand of God seized her; for one morning a terrible thunder-storm came on suddenly, she alone was struck by the lightning, and reduced to a handful of ashes in the sight of a vast multitude!

Learn, then, ye women, and be instructed by this terrible mark of God's anger. Shun all those who, by means of idle chatting and such abominable irreverence in church, make themselves instruments of the devil: shun those, if you do not desire to bring down God's direst chastisement upon your head.

§. 5.

FOR TRADESMEN AND ARTISANS.

THE idol of our days is *self*-interest, and oh, how many prostrate themselves before it, offering to it, at all times, and in all places, their most fervent homage! And thence it comes, that running after this idol they forget the true God, and eventually precipitate themselves into an abyss of evils where they shall remain for eternity, deprived of all comfort and of all love. Alas! alas! how miserable is their condition, and how widely do they differ from those who, as the royal prophet tells us, in the first place, seek God, who will shield them from every misfortune and cause them to abound in all true happiness! "They that seek the Lord shall not want any good thing."[*] This is clearly verified in all those

---

[*] Ps. xxxiii. 11.

who, before applying themselves to their ordinary business, make it a rule to assist every morning at holy Mass, as the incident which is related of the three merchants of Gubbio will show.

Those three traders went to a fair held in the town of Cisterno, and after disposing of their wares, two of them began to speak of returning home, nay, resolved to start next morning at daybreak, in order to be back in their own country before nightfall. The third, instead of consenting to their arrangement, remarked that next day being Sunday, he could not think of commencing the journey till he had heard holy Mass. If, therefore, you wish for my company, said he, you must first assist at the holy sacrifice, and when we have taken some refreshment we can start together. Endeavouring to induce them to follow his counsel, he remarked that in case they were not able to reach Gubbio that night they had no reason to be disquieted on that head, as there were several good inns on the road. All his remonstrances, however, were of no avail; for his two companions, who were bent on reaching home that night, contented themselves with saying that God Almighty would have compassion on them if they lost Mass on that one occasion. On Sunday morning, therefore, before the sun had risen, and without entering the church, they mounted their horses, and set out homewards. When they arrived at the River Corfuone, they discovered that it had been greatly swollen the night preceding, by heavy rains, which so strengthened the current that it beat furiously at the piers of the wooden bridge, shaking and weakening them. It was necessary, however, for our travellers to cross the bridge, but no sooner had they reached its centre, than it yielded under their weight, and they, with their profits, were precipitated into the boiling flood, where they perished almost instantly, thus at one and the same time losing their lives, money, and in all likelihood their immortal souls!

When the news of this calamity was spread abroad, the peasantry hastened to drag the river for the corses, which they at last discovered, and laid upon the bank till such time as they might be identified and obtain Christian burial. Meanwhile the third trader, who tarried behind in order to fulfil the precept of hearing Mass, had set out on his journey, and on reaching the river he beheld a crowd attracted round the two dead bodies. Reining up his horse, he halted to ascertain who they were, when, to his horror, he discovered that the corses were those of his two friends. The bystanders soon made him aware of the awful manner of their death, and no sooner did he hear the detail than he raised his hands and eyes to heaven, thanking the good God who had so mercifully preserved him from a like fate. Oh, how often and how fervently did he bless that hour in which he assisted at the holy sacrifice, to which he now most justly attributed his preservation. On his return home he announced the sad tidings, and caused the relatives and friends of the deceased to have the corses decently interred. Need we say that this frightful occurrence, and the miraculous escape of the good trader, excited in the hearts of the whole neighbourhood a lively desire to assist daily at the august mysteries of the altar? Accursed avarice (I must give free expression to my feelings), accursed avarice that tearest man's soul from God, nay, and almost deprives him of the exercise of his free will in regard of what should concern him most of all—his eternal salvation!

In order, therefore, that avaricious traders may enter into themselves, I will make my meaning more clear by availing myself of an example taken from the inspired volume. Sampson, as you are aware, was bound, but all in vain, with sinews of oxen, and strong fresh cords, which never before had been used. At last, he foolishly revealed to the deceitful Dalilah that his strength lay in the hair of his head; and no sooner was it shorn off than he lost all his unequalled strength and vigour, nay, fell into the hands of the Philistines, who deprived him of his sight, and condemned him to grind corn at a mill. Now let me ask, what was Sampson's greatest error? Was it that he allowed himself to be bound hand and foot so firmly? No. His error lay not in this, for he knew very well that all the ropes in the country were like so many gossamer threads to him. In a word, he erred by revealing the seat and secret of his strength, and allowing his hair to be shorn, for no sooner was this done, than Sampson ceased to be Sampson. Now let me suppose that a trader suffers himself to be bound by the ties of multitudinous engagements, such as his shop sales, bills of exchange, and divers negotiations, &c., &c. Does all the awful danger of avarice, which God so abominates, consist in all this? Certainly not in all this, but the danger lies in allowing the hair to be shorn. I explain myself. Imagine a trader who has much business to attend to, but who hearing at early morning the bell inviting to Mass, says to himself, "Business, I must lay you aside for awhile, for I must hurry off to Mass." Such a one is a Sampson bound by his business avocations, but *not* shorn. Another trader is also bound by seven or more cords, workmen to be engaged, accounts to be paid, letters to be written, correspondents to be answered, &c., &c.—one man is waiting to be answered—another to be paid—Oh, what a multiplicity of bonds! How perplexing and engrossing! What matter, however! Sunday, or the festival of his patron saint, comes; he disengages himself from all business, and proceeds with all piety to assist at many Masses, and perform various works of devotion. This also is a Sampson, bound, but *not* shorn; for, notwithstanding the multiplicity of his avocations, duties, &c., &c., he never loses sight of the most important business, namely, his eternal salvation. But mark well what I say to you now. If you are bound by a thousand ties of self-interest, without strength to sever them—if you neglect to come forth at the proper time—if you relax your assiduity in frequenting the sacraments, and grow cold and indifferent to assisting at holy Mass—oh, such miserable Sampsons! then, indeed, you are bound and shorn.

In this case, although you may *justly* add to your gains, I warn you that the way you take to do so is *not* just, for you inflict a terrible loss on your soul, and you are guilty of a sordid avariciousness that will sooner or later treat you as Sampson was treated, till, as was the case with him, the roof shall tumble on your head and crush you. And then " whose shall these things be which thou hast provided?"*

But I think I hear you say, " Those avaricious men will never be moved by our remonstrances, if we do not address ourselves to their particular bent." Well, be it so; what is your aim? To grow rich, accumulate, and make vast profits. Here, then, is the way of compassing your end. Assist at the holy sacrifice of the Mass every morning. Let me illustrate this by the example of two traders, both of whom follow the same line of business. One of them has the responsibility of a family, wife, sons and nephews; the other is childless, although married. The former supported his family in great comfort, and all his affairs prospered wonderfully. His shop, constantly thronged with customers, made exceeding large profits, so much so that he was every year able to bank considerable sums, which he reserved as marriage portions for his daughters. The other, who, as I said, was childless, had no success in trade, was dying of hunger, and all but driven to desperation. One day he addressed

* Luke, xii. 20.

his neighbour confidentially, thus: " How comes it that you are so prosperous? God seems to shower abundance upon you; and I, unfortunate that I am, can hardly raise my head, while want, in its most frightful aspect, is ever at my door!" " I will answer you candidly, my friend," replied the well-to-do trader, "and I will call to-morrow morning and show you the source from which I derive so much worldly comfort." The morrow saw him at the house of his friend, whom he led straightway to a neighbouring church to hear holy Mass. At the conclusion of the divine sacrifice he accompanied him back to his deserted shop, repeating the same performance twice or thrice, till at last the unfortunate man said: " If nothing is required to alter my wretched circumstances but to go to Mass, I know the way to the church well enough to do without your guidance." " Exactly," answered the prosperous man, " hear holy Mass every day, and I promise you that your affairs will soon take a turn for the better." And, indeed, he spoke the truth, for no sooner had he begun to assist at holy Mass daily, than he was well supplied with work, so much so that he was, in a brief period, enabled to clear off his debts, put his house in good order, and enjoy comforts to which he had been, for many a weary day, an utter stranger.* Do you believe in the Gospel? Now, if you do believe in the Gospel, how could you entertain the least doubt of this truth? Does it not tell you, emphatically, to

---

* Surius' Life of St. John the Almoner.

"Seek first the kingdom of God and his justice, and all those things shall be added to you."*

§. 6.

FOR SERVANTS AND FARM LABOURERS.

THE great Apostle tells us, that "if any man have not care of his own, and especially of those of his house, he hath denied the faith, and is worse than an infidel."† This care is to be understood as relating, not only to their bodies, but much more so to their souls. Thence it follows, that if it would be a great impiety to deprive one's servants of corporal food, it must be a far more heinous impiety to deprive them of the spiritual aliment, and especially of the most perfect facility of daily assisting at Mass, for the loss of which no employer, however rich and powerful, can ever compensate. When God made the great covenant with Abraham, He commanded that not only he, but his entire household, should be circumcised: "He that is born in thy house, and he that is bought with thy money, must needs be circumcised."§ Here, then, is an evident proof that a good Christian should not be satisfied with attending in his own person at the divine worship (especially at holy Mass), but he should, likewise, use every means in his power to induce every member of his entire household to follow his example. So punctual was Saint Elzear, Count

---

* Mat. vi. 33.   † 1 Tim. v. 8.

of Ariano, in carrying out this divine rule, that among other ordinances established for the government of his household, he made this the principal one, that all his servants should, every morning, assist at holy Mass. In fact, he insisted that every one in his employment, male and female servants, pages and grooms, should be present daily at the divine sacrifice. 'Tis, truly, a most sanctifying custom, and one, thank God, which is observed by multitudes of pious people at Rome, where Cardinals and Prelates, with their respective followers, hear Mass every morning. Nor should you foolishly think, that the time which your servants spend assisting at holy Mass is time lost. Oh, how richly will God compensate you for it!

Saint Isidore was a poor farm-labourer, who never omitted to hear Mass daily; and God, wishing to prove how grateful the humble man's devotion was to Him, caused angels to plough his field one morning, while he was assisting at the holy sacrifice. True it is that God will not work miracles so palpable for you, but in how many different ways will He recompense your piety? You can easily draw your own conclusions on this head, from what I am about to relate concerning a poor vine-dresser, who supported his family by the sweat of his brow. This excellent man made it a rule to assist at Mass daily, before going to his work. Having gone one morning, at daybreak, to the market square, he remained waiting for some employer to give him a day's work, but, on hearing the bell of the village church inviting the people to Mass, he, according to his custom, felt sorrow for his past life, which was impious, became a most devout attendant at the holy sacrifice, at which he assisted daily (causing many to be celebrated for him in various churches), till at last, after a well-spent old age, he closed his days in peace, dying a sanctified death.

Behold, now, how liberal of blessings God is to all those who prove themselves truly devout to the holy sacrifice of the Mass. To Mass, therefore, my poor people; frequent the divine oblation, and be assured, that in this permanent devotion you will find comfort and balm for all your sufferings and woes.

§. 7.

AN AWFUL WARNING TO ALL THOSE WHO DO NOT SET PROPER VALUE ON THE GREAT TREASURE OF THE HOLY MASS.

The two great doctors of the Church, St. Thomas the Angelic, and St. Bonaventure the Seraphic, teach, as we have shown in the preceding Instruction, that the most holy sacrifice of the Mass is of infinite value, both by reason of the Victim that is offered, that is, the body, the blood, the soul, and the divinity of Christ our Lord, as also by reason of the primary Offerer, who is Jesus Christ himself. And yet, alas! how many are there who set so little value on this treasure of infinite value, that they postpone it to their most perishable and sordid worldly interests. My chiefest aim in composing this little book has been to promote the spiritual and temporal welfare of all those who will deign to peruse it; and I cherish a hope, that every one who studies its pages will be enlightened by them, and taught to form something like an adequate appreciation of a jewel whose value is inestimable. And if hitherto this most holy sacrifice has been to them a Hidden Treasure, now, that they are conscious of the infinite value which it contains, may they resolve effectually, in their innermost heart, to get possession of it by assisting daily at the holy Mass. Let me, then, in the hope of causing my words to be graven on your soul, narrate to you an appalling occurrence, which will set the seal on my poor work.

Eneas Silvius, who was afterwards Pope Pius II., tells us, that in a certain city of Germany, called Svezia, there lived a gentleman of high social position, who, after losing nearly his entire wealth, retired to a country house, for the sake of economising. Spending his time in great seclusion, he soon became a prey to the profoundest melancholy, so much so, indeed, that he was in a state bordering on desperation. While he was in this deplorable condition, the devil often suggested to him that he ought to put an end to his life, "for," said the tempter, "there is nothing for a barren tree but the woodman's axe." In this conflict of mental agony and temptations, the gentleman had recourse to a holy confessor, who gave him the following good advice: "Let no day pass without assisting at holy Mass, and make your mind quiet." The gentleman, indeed, was pleased with the advice, so much so that he lost no time in carrying it out; and in order to prevent the possibility of ever losing Mass, he engaged a chaplain, who daily offered the adorable sacrifice, at which he assisted with the most edifying devotion. Now, it so happened, on one occasion, that the chaplain went to a neighbouring village to be present at the Mass of a priest just then ordained, and the gentleman, so good and pious, fearing that he would be deprived of the holy sacrifice on that day, set out for the same village, in order to gratify his devotion. On the road he met a peasant, who told him that he might return home, as the Mass of the newly-ordained priest was terminated, and there was to be no other on that day. Deeply afflicted at this intelligence, the gentleman began to weep bitterly, repeating over and over again, " What is to become of me, what is to become of me, miserable man? Perhaps this may be the last day of my life." The peasant wondered much at this outburst of grief, and said to him: " Do not weep so, Sir, do not weep, for I will sell you my Mass. Give me your cloak and I will give you the Mass at which I assisted." The gentleman readily accepted the proposal, and having given the cloak to the peasant, he walked on to the church, where he knelt down, and said a few short prayers. He then set out for his residence, but he no sooner reached the spot, where, in his simplicity, he had made that most *absurd* and *execrable* bargain with the peasant, than he beheld the latter, who had sold his Mass, hanging from the branch of an oak, like Judas, who strangled himself in despair.

In fact, the temptation to self-murder had passed from him into that wretched peasant, who voluntarily deprived himself of the aids of grace which he might have derived from the holy sacrifice, and thus left himself an easy prey to the devil, whose malignant suggestions he was not able to overcome. Pondering on all this, the good gentleman convinced himself that his confessor had given him the most valuable remedy for resisting all sorts of temptation, and he thenceforth resolved to be confirmed in his determination to assist daily at the adorable sacrifice of the altar. From this calamity so horrifying, I would have you to deduce two truths of greatest importance; first, how abominable is the gross ignorance of some Christians, who, far from setting right value on the adorable sacrifice, treat it as a thing that may be bartered for vile lucre. Hence that impropriety of language from the lips of certain people, who frequently speak to a priest in this manner: " Will you allow me to pay you for a Mass?" Pay for a Mass! and where will you find capital for that? Where will you find any sum of money that can equal the value of a Mass, since one Mass is of greater value than all Paradise itself? Oh, ignorance the most intolerable! That trifling sum of money which you give to the priest is given to him for his maintenance, *but not as a payment for the adorable sacrifice*, which is beyond all price. 'Tis true that in the course of this work I have exhorted you to hear Mass daily, and even to have Mass frequently celebrated for your spiritual and temporal necessities, and for the repose of those who are dear to you, and yet, who knows but the devil may have put it into your head to think and speak as follows: " The priests, with their fine and specious arguments, exhort us to have many Masses celebrated; but all is not gold that glistens. They are bent on making gain for themselves, and it may one day appear that their only motive was self-interest." Oh, how grievously would you deceive yourself were you to think or speak thus! For my own part, I thank God for having led me to embrace an Institute that professes the strictest and most rigid poverty, an Institute in which we accept no alms for the celebration of Mass, for even were we offered one hundred dollars for a single Mass, we would reject them, since we celebrate all our Masses with the same intention that Christ had on the cross, when He offered to his Eternal Father that first sacrifice on Calvary. Therefore, if there be any one who can speak out boldly, and without the shadow of suspicion on such a subject, it is I, whose only object is to promote your spiritual and temporal welfare. This, indeed, has been my sole aim throughout the little work which is now in your hands; and as I close it, I would fain exhort you to realise in practice the advice I have so often given. Therefore, I beseech you, once more, to hear as many Masses as you can, and to cause many to be celebrated for you, for you will thus be enabled to lay up for yourselves an exceeding great treasure, which will redound to your advantage in Time and in Eternity.

The second grand truth to be drawn from the event already narrated, is the efficacy of holy Mass in obtaining for us every good, for delivering us from every sort of evil, and particularly for conferring on us spiritual strength to conquer temptations, be they ever so numerous and formidable. Let me then repeat—to Mass, I implore you; to Mass, if you are desirous to achieve victory over your enemies, and to see the devil and all his powers crushed beneath your feet.

There remains but one other advice, which I would impress, with all my energies, on priests, both Secular and Regular, for it relates to both in an especial manner. Let me, therefore, repeat to you, secular priests, that if you wish to obtain great fruits in great abundance from the holy sacrifice, you must hear it with profoundest devotion. I have hammered on this nail more than once in the progress of this work, but I now give it the last blow in order to drive it home. When at Mass be truly devout, and if it so please you, use this little book, and carry into practice, with all possible exactitude, what I have prescribed for you in the second chapter. Your own experience (if you adopt my counsel) will convince you that I am right, for within a brief period you shall find a wonderful change effected in your heart, and if I may be permitted to say so, you will be able to lay your hand on the immense blessings which God will send to you.

Oh, ye priests! you have good reason to dread the justice of God, if, through unbecoming haste or irreverent negligence, you violate the rubrics of the sacred rites, if you pronounce the words hurriedly, and without heeding their import; in a word, if you confound the action, and celebrate the divine mysteries without that internal and external devotion which the Church prescribes. Remember that you consecrate, touch, and receive the Son of the Most High; nor shall you be without sin, if you either omit or slur over the least ceremony ordained by the Rubric. You will find this doctrine lucidly discussed by the most learned Suarez. Hence it was that that illustrious oracle of Spain, John d'Avila, held as his unalterable opinion, that the Eternal Judge will call priests to a tremendous account for all the Masses they celebrated. On this head, he tells us, the scrutiny of the supreme Judge will be inexorably rigorous and searching, far more so than in regard of any other act of their lives. Hence it was, that when some one told him that a young priest had died immediately after celebrating his first Mass, the holy man sighed and asked: "Has he then said Mass?" and on being answered that the young priest had had the happiness of departing this life immediately after his first celebration, he resumed: "Alas, he has to render a terrible account to God, since he has celebrated even one Mass." And you and I, who have celebrated so often, how will it be with us at the bar of God's tribunal? Let us, therefore, make a holy resolution to revise (at least during our annual Retreat) all the rubrics of the Missal, and all the sacred ceremonies, in order that we may be able to celebrate, as the Church requires, with all possible punctuality. And here let me say, that if we priests celebrate with grave and devout external composure, and what is of greater moment, with great internal fervour, even laymen will be brought to hear Mass daily, and to hear it with profoundest devotion. Thus will we be enabled by God to rekindle in the hearts of the faithful of our times the fervour of the early Christians, and our good God will thus be supremely honored and glorified. To promote that honor and glory is the sole aim of this little book.

PRAYERS FOR MASS, &c.

BY THE

BLESSED LEONARD OF PORT MAURICE.

AN EASY METHOD

OF

ASSISTING AT HOLY MASS

WITH GREAT FRUIT.

A Prayer to the Holy Ghost, to be said before assisting at Mass, in order to obtain His illuminating Grace.

Come, O Holy Ghost! and with thy most sanctifying grace collect, I implore Thee, all the powers and all the affections of my soul, so that with undivided attention, and with my entire heart, I may be enabled to assist at this Holy Mass, and derive from it those blessings for which, although I confess myself unworthy, I earnestly hope, to the greater glory of God, and the welfare of my soul, through the goodness and mercy of the same, my Lord and my God. Amen.

Prayer while the Priest is saying the Confiteor.

O my most amiable Lord and Saviour, who, when bowed down by agony and overwhelming grief in the garden of Gethsemane, didst address Thyself in suppliant prayer to the Eternal Father, while the drops of Thy bloody sweat bedewed the ground; grant me grace so to recal Thy most bitter passion, that I may be excited to shed tears of heart-sprung contrition, as Thou Thy bloody sweat of grief that night. Amen.

A Prayer when the Priest ascends the Altar.

O MY most loving and meek Saviour, who, when dragged like a malefactor into the presence of Annas, didst endure the buffetings of the impious Jews, grant that imitating Thee I also may endure resignedly the insults of mine enemies, and comport myself as becomes a true Christian amid all the trials and temptations of this deceitful world. Amen.

A Prayer at the Kyrie Eleison.

O MY loving Lord! whom Peter, chief of the Apostles, did deny in the house of Caiphas; I humbly beseech Thee to give me grace to shun evil associates, so that I may never, by following their counsels or example, or the promptings of my own corrupt nature, fall away from Thee and Thine infinite goodness. Amen.

A Prayer at the Epistle.

O MOST sovereign Lord! who being led to Pilate's house by the Jews, with every sort of insult, wast falsely accused by perjured witnesses; enlighten me, I implore Thee, to avoid all the snares of my enemies, and so strengthen me by the constant practice of good works, that I may never fail to profess openly and devoutly the holy Catholic Faith, now and at the hour of my death. Amen.

A Prayer at the Gospel.

O MY most compassionate Redeemer! who, when sent back by Herod to Pilate, whose hatred to Thee was the motive of their reconciliation; grant me such sanctifying grace that I may never be terrified by the artifices of the impious; but rather draw from persecutions and temptations such encouragement that even in the midst of them my heart may not wax faint, but grow more and more reconciled to Thy most holy will. Amen.

A Prayer at the Offertory.

MY Lord and my Redeemer, who, to satisfy the justice of the Eternal Father for my crimes, didst suffer Thy divine person to be bound to the column which the stripes of the scourgers sprinkled with Thy most precious blood; grant me grace to purify my soul from its loathsome stains of guilt in that all-sanctifying stream, so that I may present it pure and undefiled in union with Thy merits to the Eternal Father. Amen.

A Prayer when the Priest washes his Fingers.

O MY most tender Saviour! O Son of the living God! who, when pronounced innocent by Pilate, didst meekly bear the yells and bloodthirsty execrations of the Jews in their implacable hatred to Thee; grant me grace to lead a sinless life amid the trials and temptations of this world; oh, grant that I may always meet the insults and outrages of my enemies with resignation and holy forbearance. Amen.

A Prayer at the Preface.

O MY most sweet and loving Saviour, who didst submit to Pilate's unjust sentence, condemning Thee to die ignominiously on the hard wood of the cross! grant me the grace, that when the last hour of my mortal term shall have come, I may, for love of Thee, feel no dread when my sentence of death, no matter how agonizing, is about to be executed; but that I may breathe out my soul in the embrace of Thy most holy arms. Amen.

A Prayer at the Memento for the Living.

O MY most merciful Saviour, who, to redeem the world, didst submit to carry the ignominious Cross upon thy shoulders to Golgotha, grant me grace so to walk in Thy divine footmarks, that I may patiently embrace the cross of the mortifications and trials of this world, and carry it resignedly for love of Thee, even unto death. Amen.

A Prayer at the Elevation of the Host.

O MY compassionate Saviour, who after being cruelly nailed to the Cross by the hands of the impious Jews, wast raised up from the ground upon it; raise, I implore Thee, by Thine exceeding great mercy, my weak heart above all the passions and cares of earth, so that my soul may be constantly fixed on Thee, remembering Thy most bitter Passion, the certainty of my own death, and the imperishable joys of heaven. Amen.

HOLY MASS WITH GREAT FRUIT. 111

A Prayer at the Elevation of the Chalice.

MY Lord and my Redeemer, who hast willed that the source of all graces should be Thy blood streaming from Thy most sacred wounds; enable me at all times, when suddenly assailed by sinful thoughts, to take refuge in the power and efficacy of thy most sacred wounds, and obtain from them that aid which will enable me to triumph over temptation during my whole life. Amen.

A Prayer at the Memento for the Dead.

MY ever adorable Redeemer, who, while gasping in agony on the Cross, didst supplicate Thy Eternal Father for the salvation of all mankind, for those even who nailed Thee to the ignominious gibbet; enkindle in my heart a most ardent love of Thee, so that at every moment of my life, in conformity with Thy divine example, I may learn to love my neighbour, and do good even to my enemies. Amen.

A Prayer at the Pater Noster.

MY Lord Jesus Christ, who with thy latest breath didst recommend Thy most blessed Mother to St. John, and St. John to her; deign always to accept my body and soul, so that with Thy holy assistance I may make great progress in the way of the Spirit and of perfection. Amen.

A Prayer when the Priest puts into the Chalice a portion of the Host.

O MERCIFUL Saviour, who, descending into Limbo, didst gladden with Thy divine presence the expectant souls of the Patriarchs; cause, I implore Thee, the efficacy of Thy most precious blood and of Thy most holy Passion to descend upon the souls suffering in Purgatory, so that being released from their direful tribulations, they may be received into the eternal joys of heaven. Amen.

Prayer at the Agnus Dei.

My Lord Jesus Christ, since many of the Jews acknowledged their black ingratitude, and wept for their awful crimes when they beheld Thee expiring in torture; grant me grace, through the merits of Thy most bitter death, that I also may weep and do penance for my heinous transgressions. Amen.

Prayer when the Priest receives the most Holy Communion.

My most merciful Lord, who, to redeem all mankind, didst permit Thy most holy Body, after it was taken down from the Cross, to be laid in a new made sepulchre; grant me the grace that my heart may be so renewed, as to be a fit abode for Thee. Amen.

Prayer when the Priest gives the Blessing.

O my Lord, most loving and most worthy of my love, who, while Thy disciples were all fervently praying in the supper-room, didst send down the Holy Ghost to comfort them! cleanse, I beseech Thee, my heart with Thy most holy grace, so that the Holy Ghost may find it a pleasing dwelling-place, and abide therein, enriching with His multiform gifts the poverty of my soul. Amen.

EXERCISES

OF PREPARATION AND THANKSGIVING FOR

CONFESSION AND HOLY COMMUNION.

SOUL that belongest to God, read and meditate these devout exercises. The more you read, and the more you are influenced by these holy suggestions, the more pleasing will you be to Jesus, and the greater will be your blessing in the world to come. If the first sentence awakens deep sorrow and devotion in your heart, read no farther for a while, but rather surrender yourself to that inspiration by which God begins to attract you and work upon you. Whenever you cannot receive sacramentally, make it a rule to do so spiritually, sighing out your love to Jesus, and desiring nothing so much as to receive Him in the adorable Sacrament. For this spiritual communion, you will prepare yourself by making the following fervent acts, aspirations, and exercises.

Before Confession.

MOURN, O my soul! for all your crimes; regard your sins as the greatest of all calamities, and do so in order that you may confess them with the proper dispositions; for you have outraged God your Father; you have insulted God who created you; you have treated with indignity God who has loved you so tenderly; you have offended God who has made you his adopted child; you have insulted God who has made you an heir to the kingdom of heaven; you have insulted God the Supreme Good—

infinite goodness itself—the source and centre of all grace; nay, you have insulted God at the very moment when He was showering blessings upon you.

Mourn for your transgressions, for you have sinned against God, who for love of you became incarnate; you have insulted a God, who in His excessive love of you was born in a manger; you have insulted a God, who even in His childhood wept tears of blood for you; you have insulted a God, who for your sake lived in misery and obscurity under the humble roof of a carpenter; you have outraged a God, who for love of you spent many a weary day announcing that holy doctrine without which you could not be saved; you have insulted a God, who has deigned to bequeath Himself to you in the adorable sacrament of the Eucharist; you have insulted a God, who agonized in a bloody sweat for you; you have insulted a God, who meekly allowed Himself to be manacled, dragged, and reviled for love of you; you have insulted a God, who patiently bore the strokes, the phlegm, and the brutality of the impious Jews, for love of you; you have insulted a God, who allowed Himself to be fastened to the column, and lashed by the cruel scourgers for love of you; you have insulted a God, who did not refuse to be crowned with brain-piercing thorns for love of you; you have insulted a God, who suffered Himself to be clothed as a mock king, and made an object of scorn and jest for love of you; you have insulted a God who bore the heavy weight of an ignominious cross for love of you; you have insulted a God, whose hands and feet were transpierced with rude nails for love of you; you have insulted a God, who breathed out his last sigh nailed on a gibbet for love of you; you have insulted a God, who suffered His adorable lips to be moistened with vinegar and gall for love of you; you have insulted a God, who in the excess of His love bequeathed His immaculate Mother to you that she might be your Mother, and you her grateful child; you have insulted a God, who died and was laid in the sepulchre for love of you, who suffered His side to be pierced by the soldier's lance for love of you; you have insulted a God—a God who by His own power arose again to life, and now is enthroned at the right hand of His eternal Father in Heaven, whither He invites you. In a word, you have insulted Jesus Christ, who ransomed you with the shedding of His blood; you have insulted your Prince, your Life, the Physician of your soul; you have insulted a God, who has sought, alas how vainly! for your love, in order to shower blessings on you here, and everlasting blessings in eternity; you have insulted a God, whose love of you has known no limit. My soul, my wretched soul! why hast thou acted thus? What evil has God done unto you? Alas, alas! why hast thou outraged His patience thus? But now, at least, begin to repent of your transgressions, and to love God. Oh, that I had always served and loved that good God, who so loved me that He laid down His life for me! My God, my love, my life, my hope! I love Thee with all the powers of my heart and soul; and I detest my sins because they alienate me from Thee. At the tribunal of penance, which Thou hast instituted, I will confess all my transgressions, firmly resolved, with the aid of Thy grace, never to offend Thee more!

Another Prayer.

O MOST adorable Trinity, and most worthy of all my love, Father, Son, and Holy Ghost, my God, I prostrate myself before Thee! Mercifully regard me, most miserable sinner, who would fain be reconciled to Thee by a good confession. But, O my God, as I can do nothing but what is bad, if unassisted by Thee, I implore Thee by the bowels of Thy tender mercy so to enlighten me, that I may remember all my sins; make me sensible of their enormity and hideousness, so that I may abominate them with all my heart! O Jesus, never-failing fountain of compassion! I approach Thee that Thou mayest wash me of all my iniquities! Sun of righteousness, send the bright beams of Thy illuminating grace into the dark recesses of my soul. Divine Physician, deign to heal Thy infirm creature. Love, that art infinite, kindle the flames of Thy love in my soul, so that it may love none but Thee. And may this confession that I am going to make be all that Thou would wish it. May it bring about in me an entire change of life, so that I may be fully reconciled to Thee, my God, my hope, my love; for Thou art indeed my Saviour, and without Thee there is no peace for this erring soul.

Prayer after Confession.

OH, that I could thank Thee as I ought, my beloved Jesus, for having, by Thy gracious power, saved me from the fires of hell. Thou hast, by the Sacrament of Penance, restored me to the inheritance of Thy heavenly kingdom. Endless, boundless goodness of my God, how can I thank thee ? But, oh, this weak heart is likely to relapse, if not sustained by Thee ; and like Judas, I too am capable of betraying Thee, if Thou wilt not guide and uphold me by the aid of Thy grace. Ah! I cannot rely on myself: assist me, therefore; let Thy hands overshadow me ; strengthen me when temptations assail me, and, oh, rather call me to Thyself, through the brazen portals of death, than let me live to insult Thee any more.

PRAYERS BEFORE HOLY COMMUNION.

AWAKE, slumbering soul, to bless thy God for all His mercies ! Remember that He became incarnate for thee. Remember that Jesus, who was born in the manger of Bethlehem, who conquered death, and who is enthroned at the right hand of His Father, is now really and truly present in the most holy Sacrament of the Eucharist. O thrice holy belief ! O greatest of all consolations ! God is here really present under the appearances of bread and wine! He, the Almighty One, is ready to take up His abode in my heart, and to become entirely mine!

Act of Faith.

JESUS, my loving God, since thou hast revealed it, I firmly believe that Thou art really and truly present, soul, body, and divinity, in the adorable Eucharist. I believe that in the most holy

Eucharist I receive that very Jesus who died, and who rose again from the dead, and that in Him I receive the eternal Father and the Holy Ghost.

Act of Adoration.

O MY soul, what art thou doing? What thoughts engross thee? Yet a little while and thy loving God will come to dwell within thee. O Lord Omnipotent! I prostrate myself in humble adoration before Thee. I adore Thee, O Jesus! in this Sacrament of Thy love. Come, Mary, my tender Mother; come, all ye angels and saints, and with me adore my Jesus. Oh, obtain for me a lively faith, and profoundest veneration, now that I am about to receive my Jesus; and now my soul thou shalt be filled with all good, since thy Jesus comes to abide in thee. He comes to enlighten thee, to unite Himself with thee, in order that thou mayest have a foretaste of that never-ending delight, which He has prepared for thee in heaven. Awake! exult, O my heart! let thy confidence grow stronger; and remember that thou art now about to obtain the gratification of all thy most fervent desires. Jesus is Almighty; He can give thee all good things. He openeth His hand, and showers benedictions on all. He is to thee a loving Father, and desires to enrich thee with the profusion of His choicest gifts. He is ever faithful to His word, and He will, therefore, bless thee with everything thou dost need. O Jesus, exhaustless mine of wealth! give me Thy graces; teach me to love thee daily more and more; teach me, O Jesus! to hope unfailingly in Thy tender mercies.

Act of Hope.

O Jesus, dearest hope of my soul! I rely with unshaken confidence on Thy divine promises. Thy most precious blood, shed for me on Calvary, is a pledge of Thy loving compassion for my poor soul. O Thou who art infinite compassion! grant, now that I am about to receive Thee, that my soul may be sanctified. Grant that all its desires may be acceptable to Thee, so that I may live and die loving none but Thee, O beauty ever ancient and ever new! Come, then, God of my heart's fondest hopes, sanctifier of souls, come and sanctify me. O my soul! what is there that God has left undone to win thy love? Did He not take flesh of the Virgin Mary? Was He not born in a miserable manger? Did He not die on the cross for love of thee? and, O miracle of love! is He not now really and truly present in the Eucharist for love of thee? He now invites thee to the heavenly banquet, to receive Him, and so lovingly does He invite thee, that His divine heart will brook no delay. O love, that has had no equal! The God of infinite beauty, perfection, and majesty desires this morning to bestow such blessings on me as He hath never bestowed on the Seraphim. He deigns, nay desires to take up His abode in my heart. He, the Almighty Lord, desires to be united with me; and thou, my soul, wilt thou not give all thy love to that God who has loved thee so tenderly?

Act of Love.

Jesus, centre of my love, God of my heart, how worthy art Thou of my love, and of all the pure affections of my heart. My God, I love thee with all the faculties of my heart and soul. Thou art my Creator, my sovereign Lord, and I love Thee more than myself; for Thou art the sole object of my heart's longings. Thou art the beginning and the end of all. Oh, that I could praise and bless Thee as the angels and saints do in heaven! Oh, that I were able, even at the sacrifice of my life, to make all mankind praise, bless, love, and adore Thee! O God, most amiable! how gladly would I spend all my days in toil for love of Thee. Inflame my love that it may be worthy of Thee. Teach me, I beseech Thee, to bless, thank, and love Thee, with that love which Thy holy Mother cherished for Thee. I love Thee, O Jesus! but do Thou in Thy goodness so strengthen that love that it may never fall away from Thee, for the sake of all the accumulated goods of this transitory world. Jesus, Thou art my treasure, my life, my hope, my bliss. I love Thee because Thou hast toiled and died for me. I love Thee because Thou alone art worthy of my undivided love. Thou art my Lord and my God, and I desire nothing so much as to love Thee incessantly, and uninterruptedly. Soul, God has created thee to love Him. Give Him, therefore, all thy love. O heart, thou knowest that there is no peace, happiness, or contentment without thy God! Sever, then, all earthly attachments, and hail the coming of thy God. Mary, mother of pure love, pray that I may love my God with all my soul and all my strength. Alas! my soul, hast thou not been the abode of vice, crime, and cold indifference to thy God? Hast thou not often and often transgressed His holy laws? Ah, hast thou not often imitated the impious Jews who crucified thy Redeemer? Nay, hast thou not surpassed them in cruelty and black ingratitude? Hast thou not by mortal sin crucified the Son of God over and over again? O my soul, now that He is about to visit thee in the Sacrament of love and reconciliation, implore Him to wipe out all the stains of thy iniquity.

Act of Contrition.

My loving Jesus, by my multiplied crimes I have crowned Thee with the thorny crown; I fastened Thee to the cross; I have drenched Thy lips with vinegar and gall; I have thrust the spear into Thy side; I have caused Thee to die. How could I be worthy to receive Thee; I who am not worthy to breathe the breath of this mortal life. I am a wretch whom the earth should swallow up—a sinner against whom heaven should cast all its thunderbolts—a criminal who deserves to be detested by all created things. But, O my God, Thou art infinite goodness! How repeatedly, alas! have I trampled on Thy blood, dishonoured Thy name, scorned Thy authority; yet not only dost Thou pardon me, but Thou, of Thy own divine will, desirest to be reconciled to me; and for an act of penance, for a tear of contrition and love, Thou cancellest all my crimes, Thou restorest me to Thy favour, and Thou makest me once more Thy friend and son. Oh, in truth, Thou art my God, infinitely kind, infinitely great, infinitely faithful, and infinitely loving! Thou art my God, an abyss of limitless glories and perfection. Oh, how transcendently great is Thy goodness in giving Thyself to me—to me a miserable sinner! Praise to Thy ever-holy name! Ah, would that I might die of sorrow for having outraged so good a God. I am heart-broken for having sinned against Thee! Pardon me, O my God! I consult not my own selfish interests; I only wish that Thou, my loving God, shouldst be honoured and glorified by me henceforth and for ever. Purify with thy most precious blood, O Jesus! this sin-stained soul, till it is made a fit tabernacle for Thy Divine Majesty. O Mary, thou comforter of the afflicted! give me tears of heart-sprung contrition. My soul, thou art about to partake of the body of the Lord Jesus. Hast thou duly considered who God is, and what thou art? Ah, though thou wert one of the Cherubim, uniting in thy own person the love felt by myriads of angels, and all the virtues of the saints, even so thou wouldst never be adequately worthy of receiving thy God.

An Act of Humility.

At last, O Jesus! the hour has arrived when Thou shalt come to dwell in the heart of one who is, alas! a vile sinner. Oh, by the bowels of Thy tender mercy, I supplicate Thee to have compassion on me, and to tolerate me! Lord, Thou art that God, before the awful splendour of whose sanctity heaven and earth fade into nothingness. Ah, how unworthy, then, am I to appear in Thy sight; but I must hasten to receive Thee, for Thou willest that I should do so; nay, Thou dost invite me, and like a son I must obey Thee, my God and my All. Let the Seraphim, let the Saints, let ever-blessed Mary satisfy for my defects and want of intense devotion. Lord, if I am not worthy to love and receive Thee, Thou deservest to be loved and received by me. Do with me as Thou willest. Render me subservient to Thy greater honour and glory; make me worthy of this greatest of all favours; supply all my deficiencies, and make this poor heart entirely Thine own. The hour has come, my soul, the long-wished-for hour, when thou art to receive thy Jesus. The King of kings, the Lord of lords, thy God, is about to enter under thy roof. "Behold the Bridegroom cometh, let us go forth to meet Him." But, O my soul! why art thou so cold? why dost thou not burn with holy desire to partake of His sacred body? Ah, should not the consciousness of His divine love and compassion kindle within thee intensest love for Him? If thou were only to receive Him once during thy life, with what fervour wouldst thou prepare for that august occasion! But, alas! now that Infinite Goodness is ever ready to give Himself to thee, thou art tepid, nay and cold at the very moment when He is about to take up His abode in thee! O my soul! would that thou wert like those pure and loving ones who longed with a burning desire for this divine communion. Would that like them thou thirsted for that all-refreshing fountain. Courage, my soul! awake!

yearn to receive thy Jesus; hunger and thirst for the Supreme Good shrouded in the sacramental veils. Awake! invite Him with tears of love, and with a heart all on fire with love of Him.

An Act of Desire.

COME, Thou, bread of angels, and satisfy the cravings of my soul; come, Thou, glowing furnace of charity, and inflame my soul with the fires of divine love; come, Shepherd divine, and guide me; come, Eternal Father, my hope, my life, my joy, and source of all my happiness; come, Thou, dearest object of all my aspirations; come, Thou, comforter of the sorrowful, light supernal of the soul; come, Thou, who art the solace and refreshment of the weary; come to me, O Thou, for whom the nations prayed, and for whom the patriarchs sighed! come to me, O Thou, the desired of ages, joy of angels, glory of the heavens, supreme delight of saints! come to me, for I yearn for Thee; come to me, for Thou hast transpierced me with the arrows of Thy love; come, delay not, for my heart waxes faint, and I feel that I cannot exist without Thee; come, O Jesus! I beseech Thee, come. Most holy Mary, behold I am going to receive the body and blood, soul and divinity of thy adorable Son. From thy blessed hands I would fain receive Him. Present Him to me as thou didst to the shepherds, and the kings who came from afar off to adore Him, and to holy Simeon, in the temple. Oh, obtain for me grace to receive Him worthily! Beseech Him to fill me with His choicest blessings; and O dear Mother! hearken to the prayer of thy suppliant child.

An Act of Offering.

O MY GOD! I offer Thee this my communion in unison with that of ever Blessed Mary, of Thy holy Apostles, of all Thy Saints, and of all the just who this day receive Thee, or who shall receive Thee in future times. My wish and intention is to make all those fervent acts of preparation and thanksgiving which are offered to Thee now, or shall be offered in time to come. I offer them all to Thee now in union with those virtues, merits, and that sanctity with which Thou, my Jesus, didst receive Thyself in the Eucharist at the Last Supper. May the Church triumphant in heaven, and militant on earth, supply my deficiencies of love, adoration and gratitude!

DEVOUT EXERCISES AFTER COMMUNION.

BEHOLD my cravings are appeased! behold all my longings are gratified! now my God hath deigned to visit me! now Jesus abides in my heart! Now I can say with the Apostle, I am no longer my own but Christ's. I no longer live in myself, but in Christ, and Christ lives in me. I entirely belong to Christ, and oh, happiness! Christ is mine. Oh, ineffable goodness! the God of Heaven has passed the portal of my lips, come into my bosom, and taken up His abode in the heart of a mortal creature, who is so contemptible, so wretched, and so unworthy! My soul, of what art thou now thinking? Thou

art now possessed of that God for whom thou hast been longing. Thou art sanctified by the real presence of Jesus, thou art incorporated with Jesus. Thou and thy Jesus are one. O marvellous and delightful union! My soul, now that thou art so intimately united to Jesus, wilt thou not address Him? Wilt thou not hold sweet converse with thy God who is dwelling in thy heart? Awake, be recollected, employ all thy faculties to adore Him, and greet Him thus:—
" Welcome, beloved Jesus, I bless Thee for having come to dwell within me. Long have I sighed for this moment. But oh, how it grieves me to think that Thou hast come to abide in a heart harder and colder than the stable of Bethlehem —a heart more replete with sorrow and affliction to Thee, than the rugged cross was to Thy sacred body. O Lord! what dost Thou discover in me but a heart obdurate to Thy divine appeals—a heart devoted to the perishable things of this delusive world? Ah, my God! wherefore hast Thou come to dwell in me? Let me, in the bitterness of self-reproach, say with St. Peter, depart, depart from me, depart from this body of sin, which is unfit to be the abode of Eternal Majesty, " Depart from me for I am a sinful man, O Lord." Go and reside within those sinless loving souls who pine for Thy advent. But no, O my heavenly guest! depart not from me; for if I lose Thee I am lost. O God! Thou art my chiefest hope, and I will not be separated from Thee. O Supreme Good for whom I have longed! I will clasp Thee to my

heart; and oh, may I live and die in Thy tender embrace! Mary, my holy protectress, and all you angels and saints, share with me your affections, that I may welcome as I should this coming of Jesus to my heart.

Act of Thanksgiving.

ADORABLE Trinity, one God most worthy of my love, I thank Thee with my whole heart for having given Jesus to me, a poor sinner; I thank Thee for having given me Jesus in the Sacrament of the Eucharist; I thank Thee for having invited me to receive Him; and oh, sweet Jesus! how can I ever thank Thee sufficiently for having deigned to visit me? How can I thank Thee as I ought? O spotless Virgin! O angels! O all ye blessed citizens of heaven! O all ye souls glowing with purest love of God! enable me to thank my Lord incessantly for His infinite condescension. But how far does all this fall short of the thanks due to God! Surely the thankskiving even of all heaven falls immeasurably short of what is due to an infinite God, and what is there in heaven or on earth that could compensate Him for his infinite benefits? What then am I to do, but offer, O my most sweet Jesus! Thy own love itself in thanksgiving for Thy infinite love. Let all Thy tender mercies, Thy gracious condescension, and Thy attributes, which are infinite, render unto Thee that honour and gratitude which Thou so eminently deservest. O adorable Trinity, one God! I thank Thee through Jesus, and do Thou, O Tri-une God! thank Jesus for me. Now let my heart overflow with gratitude, and may Thy divine Majesty accept, and be content with this infinite thank-offering. O supreme and everlasting Good! to Thee alone be praise, adoration, and glory, from all creatures through endless ages. Amen. Of what art thou thinking now, my soul? Art thou not a living temple, in which Thy Redeemer has deigned really to dwell? Dismiss all idle and distracting thoughts; now is the propitious moment, now is the acceptable moment for petitioning Him for the graces which thou needest, and for obtaining them from the source of all grace who now dwells within thee. Now, indeed, Heaven's gate is open, now the adorable Trinity, with eyes of mercy and love, looks down on the object of its complacency, Christ Jesus, who is in thy bosom at this moment. O my soul! waste not a moment so precious, but employ all thy energies to co-operate in this all-important affair of thy eternal salvation. But how? What sayest thou to thy God? Ah, thoughtless and contemptible as thou art, thou wouldst fain live on in thy miseries even whilst the God of all riches is abiding within thee! Wilt thou continue dumb? wilt thou let thy thoughts be distracted? Hast thou no interests to promote, no desires to be gratified? In a word, hast thou become insensible and indifferent? Dost thou not know that if thou dost not ask thou shalt not receive? Were a powerful monarch to enter thy house, and invite thee to ask favours of him, wouldst thou fail to accept such invitation? Alas, alas! we are miserable indeed, for we have not lively faith. The King of kings, the Lord of heaven's treasures is abiding within thee; thy God has visited thee; He desires to enrich thee with every grace, and yet thou remainest silent. The Infinite, All-Bountiful Being complains that His graces are not prayed for; and impatient of man's tepidity, and desiring to outpour the treasures of His beneficence on so unworthy a creature, He Himself invites us to ask. "Hitherto you have not asked anything in my name. Ask and you shall receive, that your joy may be full."* My soul thou hast received the Omnipotent Lord, a most tender and bountiful Father, a God who is ever faithful to His word, and why therefore shouldst thou be afraid? Seek Him, trust in Him, ask Him for great favours— favours worthy of thy God.

Act of Petition.

O MY loving Lord! since Thou hast deigned to visit me that I may be enriched with Thy graces; since Thou commandest me to ask them of Thee, listen to me now, I implore Thee, by the bowels of Thy tender mercy. Bestow on me, O Jesus! an increase of lively faith, hope, charity, and sorrow for my sins. Grant me humility, purity, patience, and every other virtue; cleanse me of all my defilements; change this erring heart, and

* John, xvi.

detach it from the perishable things of this world; conform it to Thy divine will, so that I may incessantly seek Thy greater glory; cause all its affections to be centered in Thee alone; let its only wish be to obtain Thy love, and never allow it to forfeit that supremest blessing. I know that grace is a wondrous gift; I acknowledge that I have not merited it; but Thou, my loving Jesus, dost merit it for me. The great God of heaven is able to confer graces exceeding great; grant me, then, this which I have implored by your passion and death on the cross; grant it to me for the love you bear to the eternal Father; grant it to me by the merits of ever-blessed Mary; by the merits of Thy Church triumphant in heaven, and militant on earth; grant it to me because Thou art infinite goodness and compassion. [*Here pray with a lively faith for the graces and favours which are required for yourself and those who ask your prayers.*] O adorable Trinity! O my most loving God accept my humble petition. Now is the moment when Thou wilt not deny Thy graces even to the most unworthy, because it is not I alone that ask them, but Thy divine Son Jesus unites with me in imploring them. Indeed, I am not worthy of Thy attention, but Jesus, who prays with me and in me, deserves to be heard. Eternal and Omnipotent Father, I base all my hopes on the promises of my Lord Jesus Christ, who has told us that whatever graces we ask of Thee in His name shall be granted to us by Thee. "Amen, amen, I say to you, if you ask the Father anything in my name he will give it to you."*

Act of Oblation.

JESUS, my loving God, Thou hast given Thyself entirely to me, and gratitude requires that I should give myself wholly to Thee. Thou hast sanctified me by coming to dwell in my heart, and henceforward I will, with Thy divine assistance, be entirely consecrated to Thee. My eyes, which Thou hast opened to the true light, shall be Thine. My ears, which have heard Thy gentle invitation, shall be Thine; and this tongue, which has been sanctified by Thy adorable body and blood, shall be Thine for evermore. Oh, may all my senses be devoted to Thy greater honour and glory; may they never rebel against Thy holy law; may my memory teem with grateful recollections of Thy goodness; may this will, which Thou hast sanctified, postpone everything to the love of Thee. To Thee I offer my body and my soul—all my senses, and all my faculties—my entire being. O celestial fire! consume in me all that is base and impure. O Omnipotent love! teach me to love Thee with fidelity, now and for evermore. Amen.

Act of Self-Oblation to be made every Morning.

MY eternal God, behold me prostrate before Thy immense majesty, and humbly adoring Thee. To

* St. John, xvi.

Thee I offer all my thoughts, words, and actions during this day; and my dearest wish is that all of them may tend to promote Thy honour and glory. Lord, I desire nothing but to love Thee, serve Thee, praise Thee, bless Thee, and fulfil Thy divine will. O eternal God! I beseech Thee to enlighten my understanding. Teach me to have unshaken faith in Thy mercy; teach me how to satisfy Thy divine justice for my many heinous sins. Grant that my prayers may obtain comfort for the souls in Purgatory, and the grace of conversion for all sinners. 'Tis my most ardent wish that everything I undertake to-day may be in union with those most pure intentions which Jesus and Mary had during their mortal term; I desire nothing so much as that my intentions should be the same as those which actuated Thy saints during their pilgrimage in this transitory world. Grant, O my God! that I may imitate their holy examples, and live the life of the just. Accept, therefore, I beseech Thee, my poor heart; give me Thy holy benediction, and grace to avoid all sin, mortal and venial, throughout the entire course of my life, but particularly during this day on which I desire and intend to perform all the works necessary to gain the indulgences of Thy holy Church, nay, and to assist at all the Masses that are celebrated in the whole universe, applying them all in suffrage for the souls in Purgatory, in order that they may be released from their torments. Amen.

How you should act after receiving the holy Communion.

As soon as you have received the body and blood of the Lord, and retired from the church, observe, as far as you can, profound silence and recollection. Remember the great work you have performed, and never forget that you have sacramentally received Jesus—that very Jesus who for nine months dwelt in the womb of the blessed Virgin Mary. During the day make frequent acts of lively faith, and casting yourself in spirit at His feet, say to Him: "Lord, have mercy upon me. O Lord! preserve me from sin, grant me the grace of final perseverance; grant me the grace of a holy death, and make my soul worthy of Paradise. Lord, send Thy blessings on my home and family, and grant that my children may grow up in Thy holy service." Ask great blessings of God; ask with humble confidence, and you may rest assured that you will obtain them all.

The Viaticum.

In every house there should be a wax candle set apart for the most solemn moment when the priest comes to administer the holy Viaticum to the sick and dying. This candle should be called the candle of the adorable Sacrament, and should be carefully preserved, and never lit except on the occasion already specified. Devotion of this sort has merited special favours from the Most High.

Conduct in the Church.

On entering the church, remember that you are in the presence of Christ's altar, and that His divine majesty is there enthroned. You are, therefore, to comport yourself with silent recollection, interior and exterior, doing and thinking only such things as are calculated to edify your neighbour, and bring down God's blessing upon you. Avoid all noise, such as unnecessary coughing, which is likely to distract others, and especially the priest, if he happens to be preaching. Spitting on the floor of God's consecrated temple is an irreverence which should be carefully avoided. On entering the church, therefore, say to yourself, I am now in the house of God, in the presence of God's throne, and it behoves me to conduct myself with strictest and holiest decorum. All my senses must be consecrated to God, for I have entered the holy place to adore and supplicate Him. Bear well in mind what I have here laid down for your observance, and never forget that God's temple is holy, and that those who profane it by thought, word, or action, provoke the anger of the Eternal.

THE END.

www.ingramcontent.com/pod-product-compliance
Lightning Source LLC
Chambersburg PA
CBHW031323160426
43196CB00007B/643